LADY DAY

LADY DAY

THE MANY FACES OF BILLIE HOLIDAY

ROBERT O'MEALLY

PRODUCED BY TOBY BYRON/MULTIPRISES

DA CAPO PRESS

A CIP catalog record for this book is available from the Library of Congress.

ISBN: 0-306-80959-1

Designed by Eric Baker Design Associates, Inc.

2 3 4 5 6 7 8 9—02 01 00

Published by Da Capo Press
A Member of the Perseus Books Group
www.dacapopress.com

For Jacqui, Connie, and Sharon

•   •   •

We gratefully acknowledge the efforts of
Linda Lipnack Kuehl, whose inspired research proved
invaluable in the making of this book.

Contents

· · ·

Introduction

. . .

*T*his is a book about the greatest jazz singer in history. Charting Billie Holiday's rise not as a social phenomenon but as the story of an artist, it provides a critical framework for her music. She started out as a fresh-voiced young girl who, in the tradition of Bessie Smith and Louis Armstrong, boldly turned whatever material she confronted into her own music. By the time she was twenty-two years old, she had put together and recorded a songbook that included "What a Little Moonlight Can Do," "Miss Brown to You," "It's Like Reaching for the Moon," "I Cried for You," "Billie's Blues," "I'll Get By," and many other songs that we associate with no one except her.

The 1939 recording of "Strange Fruit," that mournful song of protest against lynching, marks the beginning of her middle years, during which— along with the ballads and "rhythm songs" (as Teddy Wilson called them) of the first years—she began to present the slow and dramatic plaints and torch songs that also are definitive Holiday works: "Yesterdays," "Some Other Spring," "My Man" (the Decca version), "Lover Man," and "Deep Song." It was also during these productive middle years that Holiday did a stunning series of recordings in honor of her mentor, Bessie Smith: "Ain't Nobody's Business" and "Pigfoot and a Bottle of Beer" were among these masterworks.

From 1952 to 1959, Holiday recorded dozens of titles for Verve Records. When these last years rolled around, her voice was not what it used to be. Her range had narrowed and deepened, and much of the sparkle and buoyancy were gone. But she continued to develop as an artist, and by the 1950s, she had more artistic arrows in her quiver. In a voice that was so edged with emotional

Holiday, 1945. This, the most famous of the Holiday photographs, was taken by Robin Carson at his studio in New York. For that session, she obliged Carson's request for something special by singing "Strange Fruit" a capella. "This was one of the most unbelievable evenings in my entire life," Carson told someone right after the shoot. "I'm quite sure I've gotten some beautiful pictures." (facing page)

intensity that at times it seemed unearthly and almost too much to bear—and then again was more fascinatingly playful with the sense of time—she remade many of her previous successes. These revisions of herself were in virtually every case more nuanced and evocative than the originals. As her filmed performance of "Fine and Mellow" (1957) wonderfully demonstrates, when she was well enough to perform at full artistic capacity, she was stupendous. For me, contrary to the popular wisdom, her last years were her greatest.

This is not a full biography; there is not enough space here for the comprehensive telling of such a varied and complex life. (This is a biographical essay in which the central point is that, however fascinating or instructive we may find the details of Holiday's life as a case study of the drug addict, the mistreated woman, or the African American scapegoat, in the end what matters most is that somehow, out of whatever her personal history might have been, she was able to invent for herself a shining identity as an artist.) We have been so mesmerized by the recital of this singer's private woes that at times we have lost sight of the real reason that history cares about her at all: the lure and spiritedness of her voice, her way of turning bad songs into good or even great songs, and her way of transforming already great songs into music and poetry that will last forever.

Holiday, 1935 and late 1940s.

Some otherwise very dependable music historians have been shockingly confused on this matter of Holiday as artist and have persisted in presenting her art as if it were little more than data in a psychological or sociological profile. To support their case, they quote the singer herself: "Anything I do sing, it's a part of my life." They quote musicians who knew her well: "Billie never sang a note she had not lived" or "There's a whole life in that voice." Both Holiday and her colleagues speak the truth when they say that her art is rich with palpable, dramatic, lived experience. There can be no doubt that she always knew, sometimes with painful intimacy, whereof she sang. But most critical treatments of Holiday stop right there: she was a natural; she sang her life. Then they rush to the retelling not of her training as a singer, her artistic foremothers and forefathers, or even her evolving techniques or styles as a vocalist, but instead of her sad times in "the ghetto," in jail, or in the rock-and-hard-place spaces that defined her life on drugs and with no-good men. Who, if not Billie Holiday, these critics seem to ask, is the top candidate for the most pitiable black victim in the United States, if not the world?

Of the other parts of her life—the cosmic loneliness, the fatal attraction to drugs and monstrous men, the arrests—what is there to say? The key point is

Holiday, late forties and mid-fifties.

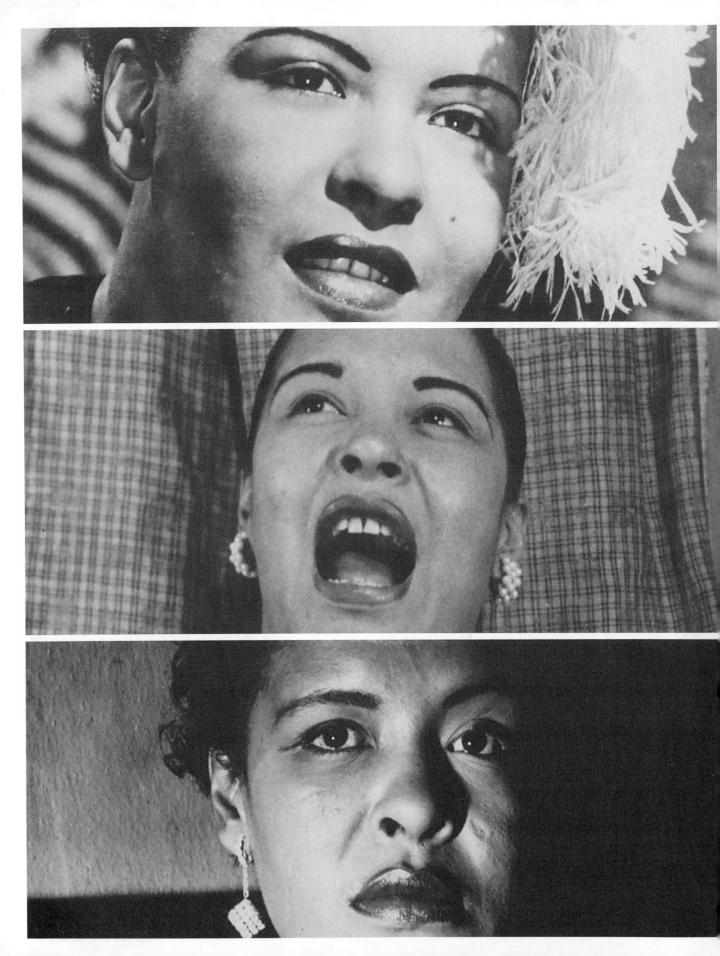

that her greatness as a singer did not derive—as many people seem to believe—from her having been an addicted and abused woman. She *was* addicted and abused, but she was many other things as well. Musicians who knew her have said she loved to laugh without holding back and that for many of her recording sessions, from the thirties to the fifties, she was bubbling over with the joy of being with friends and improvising beautiful music with them. She was not the woman on the stool holding the glass of gin and looking downcast and pained. Or she was not *only* that figure, even at the last. Like any real artist, she transmuted what she could use of her sorrows into the pure gold of her singing. She became an artist not because she was in trouble (it takes more than a sad heart to sing a sad song effectively), but because she worked hard to achieve her artistic voice and to master the timbres, turns of phrase, timings, and thousand other nuances that made her a singer whose records live on.

The purpose of this book is to show the many faces of Billie Holiday, musician. Its primary focus is on her achievement as a jazz singer and on the ways in which she developed her artistic skills. To begin with, she was the daughter of Clarence Holiday, the standout rhythm guitarist with the Fletcher Henderson Orchestra at a time when that group was the envy of the jazz world. Even Duke Ellington has said that in those days, he wished he had a band that sounded as good as Henderson's. Billie Holiday grew up in Baltimore and came of age there during the 1920s, when it was, as far as jazz talent was concerned, one of the richest cities in the nation. Eubie Blake, Chick Webb, Elmer Snowden, and Clarence Holiday were only the best-known of the jazz-playing Baltimoreans. In after-hours clubs called good-time houses (Baltimore's version of the Deep South's juke joints), these musicians and others who never left the city or had a chance to record would hold forth, night after night. It was in such places, and at private parties and in dockside bordellos, that thirteen- and fourteen-year-old Billie Holiday (then known as Eleanora Fagan or Eleanora Gough) served the first part of her apprenticeship as a singer who sang along with records by Bessie Smith or Louis Armstrong and traded choruses with piano players.

Young Billie Holiday's mother, Sadie Fagan, moved to New York for a better job and eventually sent for Billie to join her. If nightlife Baltimore provided Holiday with the hard-knocks equivalent of a high school and then a college degree in music (her formal schooling had taken her no farther than the fifth grade), then Harlem of the 1930s gave her graduate degrees and postdoctoral training. She never learned to read music (routinely, she would tell musicians who asked her for her key just to listen and follow her), but night after night in

New York, sometimes in the company of her father, she was an active participant in one of the most vibrant jazz scenes in the world. With other top musicians who had come to the city at that time, she jammed in after-hours joints and moved from club to club, working for tips. Sometimes she sang to the accompaniment of the house piano player; eventually she worked the clubs as part of a group of performers that included her own accompanists. By 1933, Holiday had packed a lot of living into her eighteen years. That was the year she was spotted by Vanderbilt heir John Hammond and cut her first record as part of a studio group led by Benny Goodman, then on the verge of public prominence. Two years later, she not only made a movie as the singer with Duke Ellington's band, but she also began the monumental seven-year series of recording dates with Teddy Wilson.

Billie Holiday's life was a tragic but unending quest for power. She sought the power to free herself from the narrow set of expectations offered her as a poor black girl born into a family where being a "bastard" child was considered an embarrassment. As a teenager, she took to the streets of Baltimore and selected a family of her own with which to identify. The hustlers and other night people of the after-hours scene at least had the virtue of admiring her musical talent and making available opportunities for her to hear, and eventually perform with,

Holiday with Ray Ellis, arranger of the *Lady In Satin* sessions (left) and in Europe with Carl Drinkard and others. (right)

excellent musicians. By the time she was thirteen, she had destroyed all roads to middle-class success and set her feet firmly on other, much harder roads.

She did not know then that she wanted to be a professional singer. All she knew was that she liked to sing and that singing won her a certain status among her older friends. She also found that singing made her happy (her friend and protégé Carmen McRae has said that she was only really happy when she was singing) and gave her more power than any of her nonmusical friends seemed able to comprehend. It gave her the power that poets have sung about for millennia: the power to remake the world and carve her signature into the job. Her life of forty-four years was so short (though she packed much into it), but her art was so powerfully long.

Why did she choose as lovers rogues such as Louis McKay and John Levy? Why did she tear up her body with heroin and whiskey? These questions, despite this book's announced focus, haunt my analysis. The drug question is an easy one. Drugs, as Albert Murray has explained, were an occupational hazard in the world where she lived. She started snorting heroin not because she hated herself or because her first husband, Jimmy Monroe, compelled her to do so. These, I believe, are among the folktales that proliferate about this fascinating woman. Monroe was the most benign of her long-term lovers—an international playboy

Holiday with Willie Smith and a friend at the Downbeat Club, New York City, late 1953. (right)

and impresario who was more enthusiastic about the project of helping Billie Holiday to dress and comport herself like a star than about the prospect of controlling her. She seems to have first tried heroin because she thought it was just another way to get a thrill, just a stronger marijuana. Like many heroin addicts, she never dreamed that she would be unable to get the drug monkey off her back.

The issue of Holiday's no-good men is much more complex. Surely her choice of tough, streetwise operators, some of them musicians, had a lot to do with her father's example. Doubtless she saw in them something of Clarence Holiday's carefree romantic playboy and flamboyantly aristocratic traveling man. Perhaps, as some people who knew her have suggested, she kept neurotically choosing men who would reenact the desertion of her father. She called her boyfriends and husbands "Daddy" and perhaps derived a measure of satisfaction from being with an iron man who would make every decision for her and who, in the face of the turbulent realm through which she moved, could offer plain and simple terms of order. And perhaps this woman with vivid memories of her Catholic girlhood — who might have blamed herself not only for her mother's unhappiness and ultimate breach with her family but even for the death of her great-grandmother, to say nothing of the later "crime" of singing the blues in all-night dives and good-time houses — derived some pleasure from the pain of being physically punished by her men.

Still, I think it is crucial to remember that at first she chose tough-guy pimp/lovers as part of a barely conscious design to win access to the night world, which she perceived as the only real alternative to the straight world represented by her mother and family. In other words, the men were part and parcel of her plan to increase her freedom of movement and her freedom to redefine the values of her life; they were part of her plan to increase her personal power. With a tough guy in tow, she could stay out all night and have protection against anyone who might wish to try something that she could not handle with her own fists or the razor she carried in her stocking. When the men failed as her protectors, as Jimmy Monroe seems to have done, she got rid of them. She would put up with their overbearing behavior and greed, but she made them keep up their end of the bargain or get lost.

The drugs made her desperate every day of the year, and often sick, as she waited in a sweat for her fix to arrive or tore through the streets trying to get it herself. And the fragile deal with her men fell apart. Those whom she had in a sense hired to free her and protect her began to tyrannize her, virtually to enslave her.

Holiday at the Café Society, 1944. Left to right: Dorothy Donegan, Holiday, Irene Kitchings, and Kenny Clarke. (preceding overleaf)

Advertisement, late 1940s. Joe Glaser, Holiday's agent, won top jobs for the singer with ads like this one. It gave misinformation about where she began her singing career—she had been singing in Baltimore and then all over Harlem before she started at Jerry Preston's—but it made clear that she was a star who expected to be highly paid. (facing page)

Lady
Sings
the
Blues

**BILLIE
HOLIDAY**

With William Dufty

One thing bedeviling any efforts to make a clear case about the life and art of Billie Holiday is that she attracted so many myths. Even her autobiography is not a dependable source of information. Pieced together from interviews granted over the years and from conversations between the author, William Dufty, and Holiday herself, that book is best considered a dream book, a collection of Holiday's wishes and lies. That is not to say that the book is not valuable, only that it must be interpreted, like other dream and wish books. Billie Holiday herself seemed to regard such accounts primarily as publicity and as opportunities to secure quick cash.

The story that she did care about was in her music. That is the story she would fight you over. That is the story, or the set of stories, that this book tries hardest to read.

Which brings us to the book's title and subtitle. Their purpose is to suggest that there were many Billie Holidays, more than we generally have taken into account. She presented several different faces to the world. She was the singer whose sound changed dramatically as the decades went by. She was the "Lady" of the dream book autobiography and of the other works based substantially on it, including several plays and a Hollywood film. She was a woman of contradictions: a victim who could be a brutal victimizer; a strong woman whom many people found pathetically vulnerable; the gorgeous "Lady Day"; the "Lady in Satin" who cussed a blue streak and, if crossed, would fight like a man. Any selection of photographs of her suggests this woman of many faces. All of them were Billie Holiday.

What intrigues me most about the idea of *The Many Faces of Billie Holiday* as a subtitle is that her faces were made up, invented; they were among her compositions. In a real sense, too, her songs were confrontations—incredibly daring and creative facings of her musical material and its traditions, her art form, and her fellow musicians and audiences, present and future. In the roles she created through her music, she faced the world not as a victim, but as a towering hero. Through her music, with its elegance and subtly dynamic artistry, she faced down a world full of trouble. And somehow in these saucy meetings with trouble, in these magnificent songs, she managed to secure the power she so desperately sought. Indeed, she discovered a power more rare and complex than anything she had at first imagined possible: the power to create and, with her creations, capture and keep an audience's deepest attention. In art she found the power to move the world.

obby Henderson had quit high school in 1931 to play piano at Harlem parties for seven dollars a night — not bad money during the Depression. He recalled first meeting Billie Holiday that year at Basement Brownie's, where she was the featured singer. Brownie's was a rather well-concealed after-hours club, a tiny, down-the-backstairs flat on West 133rd Street in the heart of what everyone called Jungle Alley, New York's jumpingest strip for swing music in that period when dark, secret Harlem was in vogue. Dot Hill, the lanky stride pianist whose stomping two-beat style made Henderson say she "played like a man," was Brownie's house piano player and Holiday's lone accompanist. Finding out that Henderson, who had come in with a group of musicians, played piano, Dot Hill invited him to play a tune.

"No," he said. "I came here to listen to you." But eventually he did work his way over to the piano and sit down.

Holiday was standing near his left hand. Someone introduced them. He took another look at her, expecting her, as a singer, to do the usual thing and ask him to play a song she knew so that she could take a few choruses on it. She was not dressed with flashiness or flair — all that would come later. Only sixteen years old, she carried herself with such maturity and such an air of urbane sophistication that Henderson was sure she was older. "I saw this well-built girl over there," he later told an interviewer. "She was a woman. 'Cause Billie, boy, she was well-groomed, man; she was a *woman*. She was the kind of woman you would admire. You would say she was statuesque."

To Henderson, the first remarkable thing about this alluring young singer was not that she could sing, but that she did not ask him to play anything for her to sing. She just said, "Well, what you going to play, Bobby?"

"'Sweet Sue,'" he said, naming a pop number of the day. To strut his stuff in a dark house where not only the highly respected Dot Hill and now this new Billie Holiday, but anyone—perhaps even his idol Fats Waller, stride king James P. Johnson, or that always formidable piano "gladiator" Willie "The Lion" Smith—might walk in at any time, Henderson played "Sweet Sue" in a rocking Walleresque style, steady and glittering with his prettiest arpeggio flourishes. On the second chorus, he interjected a quick turn of phrase he had recently worked out. He later said, "I did some trick in there that was supposed to be so hip at the time." Looking back from the vantage point of thirty-five years, Henderson remembered the "Sweet Sue" trick of that night as "so square, so hayseedish."

"Hey," said sixteen-year-old Holiday. "Do that again."

"What?" asked Henderson, looking again at the girl-woman at his arm.

"What you just did," she said.

So Henderson went over the second chorus again, just as Fats Waller had often done for him when he had found one of Waller's intricate fingerings confusing. He got to the place where he had put in his special trick.

"*That's* what it is," she said with a satisfied smile.

Before hearing Holiday sing a note, Henderson could tell from this encounter that she was not just another singer. She had stood back and listened while he had told his story on the keyboard. He had used a well-known tune as his vehicle, but she had spotted his personal variation on it. She was listening to the music in precisely the same way as a hip instrumentalist would. As the saying of the day went, "She had *ears.*"

By after-hours standards, at 2:00 A.M. the night was still young. There was more than enough time for Henderson to play a request or two for Holiday. No one can remember exactly what she sang, but chances are it was something from the Louis Armstrong songbook. Night after night in Harlem, she had done pop tunes such as "When You're Smiling," "All of Me," or "Georgia on My Mind," songs on which Armstrong had worked his magic.

It had seemed to Henderson that all the "girl singers" in Harlem were imitating the high, clear cadences of Ethel Waters. But here was someone who definitely was *not* a Waters protégé. Holiday reminded him of Armstrong, but then again she had her own timbre—now wine-dark, now scalpel-bright—

Bessie Smith, 1929. (facing page)

and she put her own spirited twists and turns into Armstrong's old songs. Yes, this girl had something different. Right from the beginning, Holiday and Henderson flirted and exchanged witticisms, all through their music.

That first night they barrelhoused with a gang of young musicians from Brownie's over to Dickie Wells' Clam House, also at 133rd in Jungle Alley, and then on to other all-night spots, perhaps to the neighborhood's Hot Cha or the Yeah Man. In a few days, they were a team, and they played together all over Harlem after their regular gigs. Soon after meeting Holiday, Henderson landed a job at Pod's and Jerry's Log Cabin (168 West 133rd Street), also just called Pod's and Jerry's, the Log Cabin, or, officially, the Catagonia Club. Noted for fried chicken and piano players, Pod's and Jerry's was a well-known Jungle Alley den where Willie "The Lion" Smith (who had recommended that Henderson be given the job) had been the house pianist before Henderson stepped in. After the stint at Pod's and Jerry's, Holiday and Henderson took paying gigs together at the Alhambra Grill on Seventh Avenue and then at an even smaller but equally jumping place, Monette's, named after its owner, the blues singer Monette Moore. Monette's was a deep-shadowed speakeasy frequented by John Hammond, then in his early twenties. But let's not get ahead of the story.

· · ·

As a teenager in Harlem, at least two years before she was "discovered" by the record and movie industries, Billie Holiday possessed a sound of her own and a strong sense of herself as a top musician. Her flowering talent and well-earned reputation as one of the jazz town's boss jazz players won her a quick and loyal following among the jazz cognoscenti and gave her career a steep angle of ascent.

Her first records, cut in 1933 when she was eighteen, show that her style was already substantially formed. Even at that time, something about the teenager's sound could make a busy club's waiters stand stock-still to listen. What made her performances so riveting and unforgettable?

Musicians like Henderson have reported that what was so attractive about Holiday the musician was that she operated not just as a soloist projecting an isolated "vocal refrain" (to use a recording industry phrase of the period) but as a full-fledged member of a jazz ensemble. "She had ears"—that is, she listened with intimate understanding to the other players. When her turn came, she improvised comments (with her music) on their musical statements, weaving

Nightclub scenes in New York, c. 1930. As a teenager, Holiday appeared in Harlem clubs with bassist George "Pops" Foster, dancer Charles "Honi" Coles, and singer Laurence Jackson. The traveling floor show moved from club to club, working for tips. Youngsters Holiday and Jackson (who at the time sang with a clear soprano voice but would later rise to fame as "Baby Laurence," the rhythm tap dancer in the Honi Coles tradition) gained valuable professional experience. (facing page and overleaf)

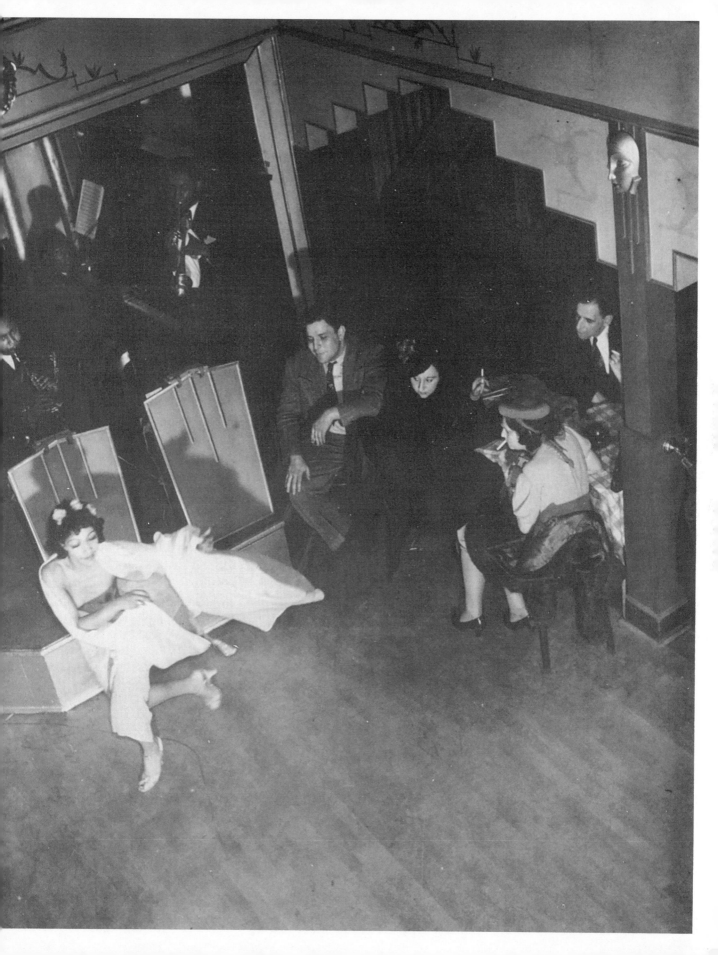

into a piece's fabric her own musical colors and rhythms. Whether with just a piano, with a full rhythm section including drum, bass, and guitar, or with larger groups including brasses and reeds, Holiday fit beautifully into the give-and-take setting of the jazz ensemble.

Examples of the tight rapport between Holiday and other musicians may be found anyplace in the Holiday canon. For especially marvelous examples of it, listen to "It's Like Reaching for the Moon," where Harry Carney's smooth carpet of thirty-second notes (on clarinet—rare for Carney, whose fame with Duke Ellington's orchestra stemmed primarily from his sonorous baritone sax work) provides the perfect foil for Holiday's sustained notes of yearning, of reaching, as with outstretched fingers, for the faraway "moon" of love. Or hear and see the Holiday of 1957 listening with enraptured concentration to her fellow players (to call the assembled studio band of Coleman Hawkins, Ben Webster, Lester Young, Roy Eldridge, Gerry Mulligan, and others "accompanists" would be a crass misnomer) on "Fine and Mellow," her outstanding performance on the classic television special "The Sound of Jazz." In both instances, what we get from Holiday is not virtuoso solo work in the one-woman show sense, but sets of choruses that fit beautifully into the overall statements. What made her so great was that her conception of jazz singing was the same as the top instrumentalists' conception of jazz playing. Theirs was an organic art in which the connections—musician to musician and musician to dancers and others in the audience—were vital linkages that meant more than any dry displays of virtuosic technique.

A typical Holiday performance was one without such exhibitions or tricks—no false smiles, no extraneous jokes, no vaudevillian patter. She came out onto the stage, she sang, and then she left, sometimes with the house going

dark while she made her invisible disappearance. If applause demanded (and if she felt like it), she offered encores. Then she bowed and left again, this time until the next show. In this regard, her performances counterpointed sharply the popping-eyed minstrel-style images from contemporary movies and radio with her own images of artistic concentration and dignity. Her performances might well be classed with those of the ever-elegant Lena Horne, Duke Ellington, Jimmie Lunceford, and Count Basie. At the same time, Holiday was a forerunner of both the Miles Davis style of "coolness" and the cool period in jazz, as well as of John Coltrane's unsmiling intensity of somewhat later years.

Holiday's was an art of minimalism. Listeners of the thirties, including musicians, report what a downright shock it was to see the very young Billie Holiday take over the stage of a small nightclub with no more than a serenely ironic look, as she waited for all the attention to focus on her. What a jolt, then, to observe this very tall-looking (she was only five foot six, but her long torso and short legs gave her an extremely tall look, especially on an elevated stage), curvaceous young woman start a song in her miniscule bell of a voice. Even in the earliest recording years, when her vocal range was at its maximum, she could comfortably sing only about an octave. "In her prime," writes Gunther Schuller, her range "could be stretched from F below middle C to the C one octave above, but in general she felt most comfortable between G and A."

She was never a belter like her idol, Bessie Smith, who came up shouting above bands under huge outdoor tents to crowds sometimes numbering in the thousands and then projecting with great force into the dull ear of early recording machines. Holiday was a microphone singer. She had come of age, artistically, at a time and in places where she was not expected to shout above a band or a roomful of noise, but instead almost to whisper her lyrics as she moved from

table to table in speakeasies. She was uniquely prepared for the era of radio and the fairly advanced microphone. Whether in clubs or on recording dates, she continued to deliver her lyrics as if only for one or two listeners whom she addressed face to face. She was quick to learn that even when she had to project above the sound of Basie's band at the crowded Savoy Ballroom in Harlem or at the Apollo Theater, the trick was not to holler but to sing directly into the mike. Although she was not one to use the portable stage mike to project a song as a "big whisper" (this was the kind of facile fakery that she abhorred), her singing did require listeners to adjust their ears for art in studied miniature. It was jazz singing of incredible spareness and economy, of embellishment without the glare of a grandly electrified candelabra but with instead the light of a single searing candle. Her singing style, one writer said, was "as fiercely concentrated as an oxyacetylene flame."

Holiday's intensive style was not without its doubters. Some charged that she was not a singer at all, that she had no voice. For them, a voice was either the big-toned socking of the blues divas or the trilling of opera-trained contraltos. Ethel Waters, never a Holiday rooter, was one of those who reportedly said that Holiday was not a singer, that she sounded as though her shoes were tied too tight. And yet those who came to mock, as the expression goes, stayed to praise. "You never heard singing so slow, so lazy, with such a drawl," said the Apollo's Ralph Cooper. "It ain't the blues. I don't know what it is, but you got to hear her."

Not unlike the poet William Carlos Williams, whose modernist poetry held to the classic standard that every word be so well placed that any change at all will alter a poem's meaning, Holiday made her few notes count *a lot*. Every true jazz work may be likened to a poetic drama, with its ensembles speaking as choruses and its solos and duets presenting dramatic soliloquies and dialogues. As a minimalist poet/singer, Holiday showed her connections to Bessie Smith. In one writer's words, "Bessie, too, had a limited range—indeed, much more so—and became a master of delivering entire blues performances within the range of a fifth without any sense of limitation." There can be no doubt that Billie Holiday much admired "the direct and sturdy simplicity of such an economical, almost recitative-like approach."

Through the necessity imposed by her limited vocal range (for "necessity," as Lester Young once quipped, "is a *mother*") and empowered by Bessie Smith's example, Holiday would strip songs down to their bare essentials, using at times only a half dozen tones to put together an entire piece. Working with such starkly limited artistic materials, and doing so with the expertise of a master painter who decides to do a sketch with one or two colors, Holiday lured the listener into her tight emotional orbit. Once she set a pattern for a song, any change at all—even an unexpected half tone up or down or a twist on a word or part of a word—could take your breath away. No wonder she inspired so many poets to write about her; in her own way, she was a poet herself.

Holiday and Ella Fitzgerald admired each other's utterly different styles. Fitzgerald recalled, "Once, when we were playing at the Apollo, Holiday was working a block away at the Harlem Opera House. Some of us went over between shows to catch her, and afterwards we went backstage. I did something then, and I still don't know if it was the right thing to do—I asked her for her autograph."

Holiday at Carnegie Hall, 1948—her first show after a year in jail. To accommodate the sellout crowd, the promoters let fans sit on the stage. She was in great form and the audience went wild, stamping and whooping until she came back for six encores. With her are (left to right) Bobby Tucker, Remo Palmieri, Denzil Best (hidden, on drums), and John Levy (the bassist, not the boyfriend).

It is often forgotten that words were Holiday's medium almost as much as notes. "The lyrics," said Carmen McRae in an interview about Holiday, "are the most important things that a singer has to work with, because the tune—well, you can improvise on that fella any way until you get it just the way you want it. Your words are your tools." Never much of a scat singer, Holiday was absolutely never a singer who, like Ella Fitzgerald, Sarah Vaughan, and their imitators, would sometimes act as if a song's words were nonsense sound pegs to hang notes on. More than Fitzgerald or Vaughan, Holiday used her impeccable diction to make herself into a great interpreter, often really a subtle destroyer and then rebuilder, of her songs' lyrics. To magnificent effect, she delivered her songs on a visceral as well as an intellectual level. Every note was an idea, and every idea was a comment on (if not an outright complement to) the given

song's meaning as expressed in its lyrics. In the best Holiday material, all the ideas fit together to create a wonderful musical unity: melody sustained mood, emotion sustained quality of voice.

Neither was Holiday an on-the-spot improviser in the Fitzgerald and Vaughan vein. Instead she would work out in advance all the details of how she wanted to do a song. Although she might make miniscule changes set to set, in general she would stick fairly close to her preset plan of invention. Over the years, of course, these incremental changes to a favorite song often resulted in an entirely redesigned approach to it. Even listening to Holiday's alternate takes done for a single session, where the musical variations were almost always infinitesimal, is rewarding, for the changes may have been slight but never insignificant.

What musical techniques did Holiday have at her command? What were the components of her splendidly unified performance? What elements made her what Barry Ulanov termed "the definitive modern jazz singer, after whom most significant singing styles since swing have been fashioned"? More than any other aspect of her singing, musicians and other close listeners have singled out Holiday's unfailing rhythm as the beautiful base upon which her distinctively sculpted songs were placed. Bobby Tucker, one of the best in a long line of Holiday's excellent piano collaborators, told an interviewer:

> *One thing about Lady, she was the easiest singer I ever played for. You know, with most singers you have to guide 'em and carry 'em along— they're either laying back or else runnin' away from you. But not Billie Holiday. Man, it was a thrill to play for her. She had the greatest conception of a beat I ever heard. It just didn't matter what kind of song she was singin'. She'd sing the fastest tune in the world or else something that was like a dirge, but you could take a metronome and she'd be right there. Hell! With Lady you could relax while you were playin' for her. You could damn near forget the tune.*

Martin Williams recalls hearing Holiday at Carnegie Hall in 1956. She did "I Cried for You," which by then had been a staple of her repertory for more than twenty years. For the original version in 1936, the tempo had been bright and quick, an up-tempo two/four dance. In versions of the forties, she sometimes turned it into a magnificently slow lament, a sardonic cry of revenge: "Now it's your turn to cry *over me!*" To rub in the meaning, she would sing those last words with the utmost saltiness. In 1956, however, Williams reports,

Holiday with Louis Armstrong, 1947. When she first started singing, she sounded so much like a "female Louis Armstrong" that her father said the public would never accept her. By the time she cut her first records at age eighteen, the Armstrong influence was still evident, but she already had a personal and unique style.

"she took 'I Cried for You' very fast and with such poised rhythmic sureness that she seemed to be kidding her accompanists about the speed—or paying no attention to them at all—and she did not falter." As a keeper of the time, she was as surefooted as a drummer or rhythm guitar player.

Seasoned during her years as a juke joint singer, Holiday had an incredibly poised sense of rhythm derived from settings where dancers insisted, with stomps and shuffles of the feet, that the rhythms be compelling and steady. Even if no dancers came onto the floor, the drive and play of the musicians' beats were essential to the ritual action and the poetics associated with those spaces, where the good times were invoked and blue Monday moods (pervasive every day of the week during the Depression) were two-stepped, pecked, and finger-snapped out-of-doors. Flawless rhythm, unpredictable in its angular accents and yet as steady as a heartbeat, was one of Holiday's most dependable weapons against the blues. Slow or fast, any Billie Holiday song was a drumsong.

Anyone wondering whether Billie Holiday was a serious student of Louis Armstrong's singing style should check out Armstrong's thirties version of "Between the Devil and the Deep Blue Sea," in which the opening phrases are hauntingly anticipatory of Holiday's tone, whimsicality, and sense, learned from Armstrong, that Broadway or Tin Pan Alley tunes were as available as the blues for reinvention and play. We also must not forget that Holiday was just as strongly claimed by the example of Armstrong the instrumentalist. In the words of Martin Williams, "She learned from his trumpet the deeper and more complex vehicle of his art; she took whatever aspects of that side of Louis Armstrong she needed and she made them her own. She was drawn to the greatest Armstrong, the majestic melodist poised above the beat, above his accompaniment, and above his material—but with his emotional roots planted firmly." Like Armstrong, Holiday could not only keep a song's rhythm going, but she could also play with it or against it. She could relax in front of the beat or just behind it, or she could let her voice float, like Armstrong's trumpet, over the beat being maintained in a more obvious way by other members of her group. Like Armstrong, Holiday was a highly disciplined artist whose playful dances with the music's pulses gave listeners an exhilarating sense of devil-may-care freedom within settings of what seemed to be superhuman control.

If Holiday's sparklingly clear enunciation made her an irresistible interpreter of lyrics, it also gave her a powerful set of rhythmic sounds with which to interlace her tunes. Rolling *r* and *l* sounds, flashes of *d, s,* and *t* sounds,

and well-measured, full-toned vowels infused her music with a subtly nuanced play of rhythmical beats. Lest there be any question of the truth of Carmen McRae's unequivocal assertion that Holiday could "swing you into bad health," listen to her "Swing, Brother, Swing" on the live air check from Harlem's Savoy Ballroom of 1937. On that number, Holiday's propulsive delivery of the lyrics swings the band and, one feels, the dancers as well. But also listen to the studio version of the more gingerly swinging "Miss Brown to You," with its quick, light rhythmical drive. Holiday's first records were cut for the burgeoning jukebox market, as the Depression had made the private retail record-buying market almost nonexistent. Put a nickel in the machine, that was the idea: dance to Billie's mysteriously subtle and many-tempoed songs.

Another key element in Holiday's art was her voice's timbre: its distinctive tonal quality, the way she made those hard- and soft-swung notes *sound*. Stanley Crouch has said that in her singing, one heard an apparent paradox: the rawness that was nonetheless so cultivated. Leonard Feather claimed that at its best, her voice had a taste of both "caviar and grits." What both these distinguished Holiday watchers were getting at is that her voice was small but multicolored, earthy in one instance and cool and refined in another. In Whitney Balliett's words, "She had an affecting contralto that took on innumerable timbres: a dark brown sound, sometimes fretted by growls or hoarseness, in the lower register; a pliable oboe tone in the high register; and a clear, pushing, little-girl alto in between."

Depending on the song and what she wanted to do with it, her voice could be bubbly and sparkling with good humor or husky and dark. "Getting Some Fun Out of Life" is a reveler's dance song delivered in Holiday's freshest contralto with infectious gusto and a wink of catch-me-if-you-can naughtiness as she exults, "Maybe we do the right thing, maybe we do the wrong." Yet at the same session (September 13, 1937), she could deliver "Trav'lin' All Alone"— a piece also taken at fast-dance speed for the Lindy-hopping jukebox market —and her voice is troubled in spite of the brightness in tempo. Here again, form serves meaning. The song is about loneliness and drift, and though she never comes close to giving in to the potentially maudlin, self-pitying aspect of the song—the breakaway tempos disrupt any real chance for self-sorrow—her treatment gives the song a poignancy that goes much deeper than would another singer's calls to complaint and ready tears. Crouch (with Albert Murray in mind) terms this quality "double-consciousness," a crucial element of much of jazz and one that characterizes much of Holiday's singing. It is a sad song

Holiday with pianist Bobby Tucker, c. 1947. Holiday loved Tucker's playing, and did not approve of his working with other singers. When she went to jail for a year, he refused to work with Ella Fitzgerald, Sarah Vaughan, and Dinah Washington "so as not to drag Lady."

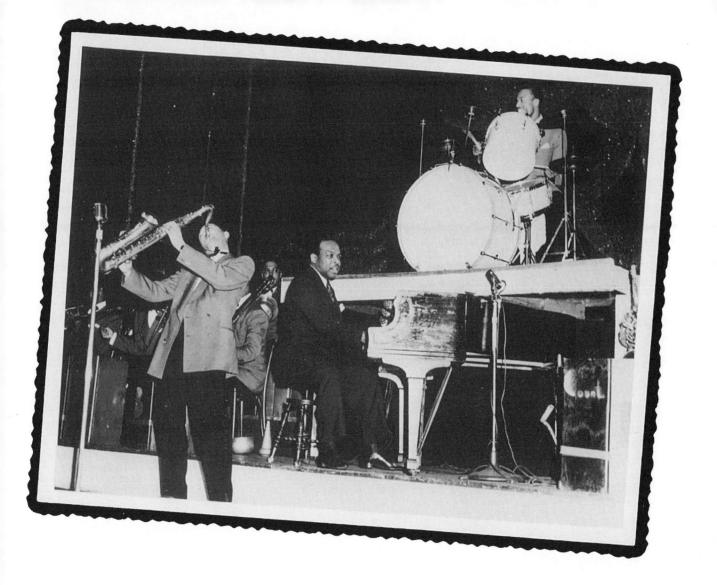

rendered with poignancy appropriate to the lyrics; nonetheless the song's sorrowful sentiments are counterstated by a tempo and an overall treatment that says forget your troubles, *get up and travel with me. Let's dance!*

In "Trav'lin' All Alone," it is not just the delight of invention or the dexterously rhythmical play and counterplay that makes one compare Holiday's performance to those of master instrumentalists such as Louis Armstrong, Lester Young, and Buck Clayton; it is also the sound of the notes themselves, the timbre. Miles Davis once commented that he would "rather hear her with [pianist] Bobby Tucker…. She doesn't need any horns. She sounds like one anyway." Holiday made the same comparison: "I don't think I'm singing. I feel like I am playing a horn. I try to improvise like Les Young, like Louis Armstrong, or someone else I admire. What comes out is what I feel. I hate straight singing. I have to change a tune to my own way of doing it. That's all I know."

I find the circling of cultural influences here fascinating. She was trying to sound like a horn, and the particular horn players she was trying to sound like were trying to sound like a singer. Whose horn was more of an extension of the singing voice than Armstrong's or Young's? Young always insisted that for jazz instrumentalists to convey the full meaning of a ballad, they must know the song's lyrics so that they can sing them through the chambers of their instruments while playing.

When Holiday was quite a new recording artist, her timbre was hornlike in its reediness. As Gunther Schuller has observed, when she was only twenty-one, "her voice was becoming heavier, hoarser, tougher, although again she could modify and brighten it, seemingly at will." Now it was a saxophone, especially Lester Young's; now it was an Armstrong trumpet, soaring and percussively lyrical; now it was an English horn, somber and clear; now it was an oboe, sadly beckoning in a thin, double-reedy voice. Through all these timbral color changes, which occurred not just from song to song but also from line to line within particular songs, her voice was small but powerfully weighted, her notes like perfectly cut diamond pendants on a simple gold chain.

Until virtually the very last, when her control sometimes wavered painfully, Holiday hit her notes dead center. She had perfect intonation. In her hitting of the notes, there was no cheating by covering up with a florid vibrato, as is typically the case with jazz and nonjazz singers alike. Where she did choose to add vibrato, it was to grant a single word or syllable (and a single note or two) added emphasis and passion. Here again was Holiday the minimalist poet in action. Generally her notes had no vibrato at all. They cut through to listeners with a slashing power that anticipated Miles Davis's similarly understated lyricism. As with every other aspect of her art, Holiday's vibrato was one of the musical colors she used to intensify her music's significance and power. In an interview published in 1959, Holiday spoke of this issue of vibrato: "When I got into show business, you had to have the shake. If you didn't, you were dead. I didn't have that kind of vibrato, and when I sang, people used to say, 'What's she putting down?'… That big vibrato fits a few voices, but those that have it usually have too much. I just don't like it. You have to use it sparingly. You know, the hard thing is *not* to sing with that shake."

Any poetics of Holiday's art must make the crucial point that while "other singers would perform or render a song, Billie would *create* one." What this means is that not only was Holiday involved in dynamically interactive relationships with her fellow musicians and members of her audiences, but the same was true of her relationships with her songs themselves. One might say that as much as any other

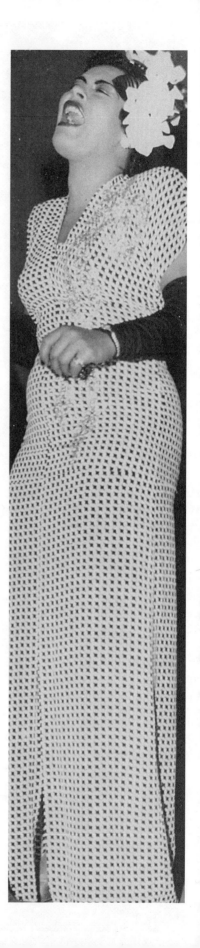

singer of this century, Holiday had an attitude vis-à-vis her songs that was comparable to the attitude of a great actress toward her lines, movements, and gestures. Holiday's art, writes Martin Williams, "was always soundly histrionic, for she had the ability of a great actress to keep a personal distance from both her material and her performance of it and to imply a criticism of it."

"She could make you *visualize* a song in a way that was just so clear," said Carmen McRae. Record producer Milt Gabler has said, "She got *inside* of a song." Music critic Ned Rorem remembered hearing Holiday in the forties and becoming so wrapped up in her performance that he wondered, "Is this person going to get through this song? She's so involved…her eyes closed, her head back. It's pure theater. It's not real life…. It's a concentration of life." As a stunning enactor of songs, Holiday pursued her task in an extraordinarily complex way. To be sure, at times she would use her gifts to deliver a song's lyrics and melody with a high degree of faithfulness to the composer's desires. Knowing her impulse and genius for creating her own songs out of other composers' material, one might be surprised to learn how often Holiday presented love songs (her relatively happy "in-love" songs) with a fairly full measure of rosiness and heartfelt yearning. There are no sunnier love songs in the world than Holiday's versions of "Easy Living," "On the Sunny Side of the Street," and "Me, Myself and I."

In the cases of "A Sailboat in the Moonlight (and You)" and "What a Little Moonlight Can Do," she delivers the mawkish lyrics with so much artfulness and conviction that she manages to strike beneath their arid surface of sentimentality and tap deep springs of hope, peace, and passion. Such cases have caused some critics to say that Holiday discovered abiding human values and feelings in songs that on the page or in other singers' hands are only corny clichés. Part of what makes her treatment of these particular songs so wonderful has nothing to do with the lyrics as such, even though Holiday the prestidigitator does make them work. As musical constructs, full of the Holiday fire of life and brimming with ideas played brilliantly off of ideas expressed by the pieces' background ensembles or other soloing musicians, these songs transcend their lyrics' meaning. But leave it to Holiday to have it both ways: she makes the songs work as pure music and somehow even makes us believe in that sailboat and "you" and even in the ooo-ooo-ooo of what a little moonlight can do! That is what makes her art completely irresistible: Holiday would not only give you personally stylized music, but she also would transform her songs' lyrics into brand-new and wonderful poetry.

It is little wonder that there was confusion, even at times in Holiday's own mind, about whether she was the actual composer of certain of her signature songs—for example, "Strange Fruit," lyrics and melody by Lewis Allen, which she often claimed to have written. Nor is it true, as she often told interviewers and audiences, that the song was "written especially for her." It was written with no particular singer in mind, and it was performed many times well over a year before Holiday knew anything about it. Nonetheless, she could be stridently adamant that no other singer should perform "Strange Fruit." For example, she was enraged at singer Josh White, who performed the song one night at the Café Society. (They finally came to an amiable agreement once White convinced her that he was not trying to steal "her song" but just wanted to do it in an entirely different way.) All this confusion arose not only because Holiday was a myth maker, but also because, while Allen's name is justifiably on the sheet music, Holiday's version of the song represents so radical a transformation that it did become, in a way, her own composition. Any transcription of one of her versions of the song would show that her treatment of its melody and harmony owed little to Allen's charts.

The outstanding trombone player Bennie Morton, who often recorded with Holiday, said, "I have seen Billie turn the melody line around completely simply because a lot of these tunes sung as written were pretty dull." On May 11, 1937, Holiday was confronted by the challenge of "I'll Get By," a schmaltzy foxtrot if there ever was one. Johnny Hodges, Ellington's incomparably lyrical alto saxophonist, precedes Holiday with a gloriously rich-toned pair of choruses in which he ascends the song's ten notes with glissandi that one writer, speaking of Hodges's playing on this song, called "creamy...like yogurt laced with Napoleon brandy." Swinging in his totally effortless-seeming way, Hodges relaxes the tune's rhythmic framework, claiming it for the province of danceable as well as listenable jazz. After such a display of control over a rangy tune by the man Ellington called his band's best singer in history, what's a Lady to do? Unfazed as usual — if anything she seems inspired to greater heights by the example of the swooping Hodges alto — she turns "the melody line around completely" and reminds Mr. Hodges who the real singer in this session is. Here is Humphrey Lyttelton's fine reading of Holiday's choruses on "I'll Get By":

> As written, the song, in F major, begins on the lower F and ascends, in
> its two opening phrases, to an upper limit of A above the octave. Billie
> Holiday starts her chorus on that upper A, and indeed hinges her

whole variation on it, with the result that, instead of soaring aloft, all the phrases droop downwards like the boughs of a weeping willow. Furthermore, apart from two descents to a low G in which her voice falls away to vanishing point, she restricts her range to a mere 6 notes.

As Lyttelton makes clear, Holiday improvises not only the melody but also the conception of the song's rhythmic pulse. Hodges loosens up the song's rigid rhythmical "skeleton"; she "cuts loose from it altogether," hovering behind the song's basic oompah patterns in a way that implies great expanses of space and leisure. According to Lyttelton, "The art of this exaggeratedly 'laid back' phrasing, distinguishing itself from mere affectation, is that the listener should not detect the point at which the performer catches up with the regular metre. The listener who expects Billie to re-orient herself by clinging, if only for a few bars, to the beat must wait, in this instance, for ever."

Here again Holiday's changes serve the song's meaning, as stated in the lyrics, shopworn though they may be: "I'll get by as long as I have you." But alongside the sentimental verbal message is the lustrously inventive and coolly poised presence of Holiday's voice, whose message seems to be, "Hey, baby, I *will* get by…*whether I have you or not!*" Her voice also is quite convincing in its awareness of the world's potential for error and trouble. Note the line declaring, "Poverty may come to me, that's true," which in 1937 was by no means a mere poetic conceit.

The oblique and yet minimally adorned treatment of the song, particularly in contrast to the direct, almost operatic flourishes by Hodges, seem to me to emphasize the smallness of Holiday's voice as well as its undying cleverness. More musically daring than even the spectacular Hodges, her voice completely *turns the song around*. Once again, it is as if we see Holiday's subtle weaponry turned to the death against the blues (i.e., the blue moods of melancholia and despair). In her hands, even the song's fatuous lyrics seem to attain something of the heroic import of blues music. Her treatment underscores the lines "Though there be rain and darkness, too/I'll not complain, I'll laugh it through." Her voice, without a trace of a smile in it, belies any easy definition of what it means that she will "laugh it through." What is suggested is a deep humor, one step from cynicism—or, as Bobby "Blue" Bland says, "two steps from the blues"—an awareness that things really might not work out. Implied is a readiness to confront life anyhow, poised for action in the face of all dismay. Thus, "Lady Day" weaves

a bit of Tin Pan Alley dross into the gold of "near-tragic, near-comic" expression (part of Ralph Ellison's definition of the blues).

It is also true, as many critics have noted, that Holiday sometimes did more than just change the emphasis of a song's meaning. At times she would use her composer's capacity to change a song's meaning to the opposite of what the original composer had in mind. Lyttelton cites the fascinating example of "Back in Your Own Backyard," with words and musical structures to support an unequivocally optimistic interpretation. Life is quite fine, the song says, and the quite-fineness is readily available, just step around your house and bask happily in happy nature, "back in your own backyard." Changing the song's brightly swooping phrases to ominously floating ones casts a pall of doubt over the romantic lyrics. "Her approach here is quite different from the dismantling and reassembling to which she subjected 'I'll Get By,'" Lyttelton writes. "The tender sadness with which Billie invests the melody imparts the rather less cosy message that we should make the best of life as it surrounds us, because it's all there is." Under the pressure of Holiday's satiric recomposition, the original meaning of the words is thrown into reverse. Once one hears the song in this way, even the now ironic word *lies* seems to support Billie's new ironicized interpretation: "You'll find your happiness lies/Right under your eyes,/Back in your own backyard."

She also works this sort of inverse melody making and reverse English on the pop tune "Things Are Looking Up." This is another song with brightly hopeful words that Holiday delivers in such a dolefully moaning style that the meaning as written is contradicted. In place of the original is a troubled song in which the truce with the down view of life is tentative and unstable. Again it is the poignant, near-tragic Holiday who undermines the simplicity of easily rhyming lovey-doviness. "Summertime" follows this pattern of undercutting prior meanings. Rather than a sweetly nostalgic hymn to summer peace, Holiday's "Summertime"—dragged out in dark colors and sinking declamatory tones—is turned into something ominously beautiful—a night-blooming flower that is at least as much Holiday as it is Gershwin.

Bobby Tucker, Holiday's pianist from 1946 to 1949, recalled that when he first began working as her accompanist, she did not impress him all that much. "She didn't kill me at all," he said, "not at all." What made the job a pleasure was playing for an audience certain pieces from the Billie Holiday–Teddy Wilson songbook that he had considered strictly Teddy Wilson tunes. What made the gig a gas was not Holiday but playing those Wilson parts he had grown up

At New York's Apollo Theater, 1937.

trying to play. One night while on a job, Tony Scott, the group's clarinetist, walked over to Tucker while the group was relaxing between shows.

"What is it you don't like about her?" Scott asked.

Tucker was taken by surprise. "There's no sound," he said. "I don't know. It's a flat thing."

"Who do *you* like?"

"Ella, Sarah, other singers, real singers," Tucker replied. And then the typical jazz musician's summary: "Of course, I don't like *any* of them, really. I just wait for them to do their stuff and then get on out the way."

"Yeah," Scott said, "a singer like Ella says, 'My man's left me,' and you think the guy went down the street for a loaf of bread or something. But when Lady says, 'My man's gone' or 'My man's left me,' man, you can see the guy going down the street. His bags are packed, and he ain't never coming back. I mean like *never.*"

"And it was true," Tucker recalled. It was during that night's second set that he "started listening to *what* she was saying and *how* she was saying. And once you start that, you can't get away from it."

Elsewhere, Tucker has been more specific about Holiday's effect on him: "We would do a tune like 'Ole Devil Called Love.' Now there's a couple of lines in there about '…rocks in my heart,' you know. And when she'd hit you with that 'rocks in my heart' line, you'd say to yourself, *'Good God, Lady, how cold could it be!?'* She would just literally tear you apart with how she could say a lyric. She could get into a lyric like no one I've heard yet."

What does all of Holiday's music add up to? What does it all mean? Maybe Stanley Crouch is right that Holiday's œuvre comprises a kind of national epic:

> *What else can one call these recordings of Holiday's? They lament, they celebrate, they philosophize, they cajole, seduce, satirize, protest, question, laugh, cry, shatter in vulnerability, or pose with stoic grace. And, since they address aesthetic problems through the medium of improvisation, they propose to give the moment something it never ʻhas—order, which is the greatest contribution of jazz: it shows over and over that the present, the most anarchic region of experience, can be given perceivable form.*

Minimalist that she was, Holiday compressed the songs she sang to suit her voice and, if Crouch is right, her rather large artistic purposes. She lured the listener into the world where she and nobody else was the deity, the Lady Day.

How did she learn this compelling art of epic statement? Most critics, even the brilliant and thoroughgoing Gunther Schuller, have referred to Billie Holiday as a natural. Others have said that she worked not by conscious design but by intuition and instinct. Whitney Balliett blandly asserts that she "came out of nowhere." This is never true of an artist, but in this case it is necessary to repeat the truism that the more natural seeming the artist's work, and the easier the artist makes it look, the more practiced and highly disciplined is the art that lies behind it. Many of Holiday's accompanists have said that she rarely rehearsed. When did she work on her craft? What did her apprenticeship consist of? How did she learn to do her thing with such authority and poise that usually dependable critics have been tricked into falling back on these lame clichés? These are the questions for the next chapter.

Holiday, 1939 at the Park Lane Hotel, New York City.

Part Two

· · ·

THE TRAINING OF A JAZZ SINGER

Jazz critic Humphrey Lyttelton has singled out an event in Billie Holiday's early life as being as stunning as almost anything else that happened to her. It is an event for the jazz history book, though so far, aside from Lyttelton, no jazz historian has noticed it.

The year was 1933, and twenty-two-year-old John Hammond, the farsighted millionaire who had left Yale to pursue his interests in jazz and leftist politics, had made his way to Monette's in Harlem. He had gone there to hear Monette Moore, the blues and ballad singer (à la Ethel Waters) who was just opening the new club. To Hammond's disappointment, Monette was too busy greeting her new clients and taking care of details to sing that first night. So with no formal announcement, the piano player, Dot Hill, simply commenced the evening's entertainment by vamping out a few block chords. And suddenly someone was singing. Hammond could not see who it was, but her voice was soft and delicate yet also forceful.

Billie Holiday's first number that night was an enticing Johnny Mercer song titled "Would'ja for a Big Red Apple?" Walking from table to table, she sang without a microphone:

> *Would'ja for a big red apple?*
> *Would'ja for my peace of mind?*
> *Could'ja for a big red apple?*
> *Give me what I'm trying to find?*

Just imagine you're my teacher
Teachin' me the golden rule
If I had a big red apple
Would'ja keep me after school?

By the time Holiday got to Hammond's table, she was singing a chorus of the "One O'Clock Blues," which he thought was thrillingly Bessie Smith–like. Later on, she did the more directly naughty song "Hot Nuts," turning her wide hips and flashing her dark eyes as she sang at a quick, light tempo. "'Hot Nuts,'" recalled Hammond, "is when I turned off because I was a guy who didn't smoke or drink and who was very pure." But still, he thought, the voice was *wonderful.*

When there was a break, he offered to buy Holiday a drink. She sat down, no doubt sizing up Hammond right away as a square. But he was friendly and very flattering. He told her that she was the best thing he had heard in years. "When I first heard Billie sing at Monette Moore's," he later told an interviewer, "I heard something that was completely new and fresh—the phrasing, the sound of an instrumentalist." In some ways, her treatments of songs recalled those of his favorite blues singer, Bessie Smith, but her vocals were more modern and forwardly propulsive in their swinging invention. The voice was smaller, but it had something of Smith's phrasing and vividness of projection. Holiday also had something of Smith's artistic raucousness, the sensation that when she sang—Watch out!—anything might happen. Holiday had something of Smith's downright *bodaciousness.*

"Who's this new girl?" Hammond asked Moore. "She's quite a talent."

"She's just Billie Halliday," Moore answered flatly. "She's Clarence Holiday's daughter, but she wants to be known as 'Halliday' for some reason. You haven't heard about her? She's all right." Moore could not conceal a twinge of jealousy. Hammond was there to help *her*, not some young heifer named Billie Whatever-it-is.

Hammond came back to Monette's every night for three weeks running to hear this exciting new singer. Then Monette's, like so many other after-hours places, was closed by the law. It reopened under a new name a few months later. Hammond wanted Holiday to consider recording the song he had heard that first night, "Would'ja for a Big Red Apple?" and maybe some blues. She must have watched him suspiciously, wondering just what he wanted from her, uneasy with his rich-boy polish. Was he slumming? Was he trying to impress her by not taking even a small drag on a reefer or a quick taste of gin? Was he for real? Who *was* this cat?

John Hammond, c. 1935.

(preceding page)

Holiday, August 1935. In the alley behind the Apollo Theater, she posed with (left to right) Ben Webster, Ram Ramirez (kneeling), a man known only as Shoebrush and Johnny Russell.

(facing page)

Though Holiday probably never read it, Hammond made a breathless announcement in the April 1933 issue of *Melody Maker:* "This month there has been a real find in the person of a singer named Billie Halliday. Although only eighteen she weighs over two hundred pounds, is incredibly beautiful, and sings as well as anybody I ever heard." At the time, Hammond's British buddy Spike Hughes also reported on "Billie Halliday": "She was a tall, self-assured girl with rich golden-brown skin, exquisitely shown off by the pale blue of her full-skirted and low-cut evening frock. Like a Gypsy fiddler in a Budapest cafe she came over to your table and sang to you personally. I found her quite irresistible."

It was during the brief stint at Monette's that Hammond introduced Holiday to Benny Goodman. At that point, Goodman had no band of his own, but he was a much sought after studio sideman.

"Benny, this is Billie Halliday," Hammond said. "Maybe we can put together a record date with her as your girl vocalist." Goodman blushed and could barely speak. Like many musicians Hammond was helping, Goodman often wished Hammond would mind his own business. For one thing, there was the problem of recording with blacks. Goodman had jammed with blacks before, but aside from a few barely audible fills on a Bessie Smith song, he had never made any records with them. "He was afraid he would lose his recording jobs," Hammond recalled. But Hammond worked on him, finally persuading him that "things weren't quite as uptight as he thought they were." And he promised that Shirley Clay, a black trumpet player Goodman greatly admired, would join them on the date. For Holiday's part, she thought Goodman was a pretty fair clarinetist, not bad for a white cat, and must have wondered why he kept staring at her and smiling.

"We'll see what develops," Goodman said. She did not seem to be everything that Hammond claimed, but she did have something. And God, he thought, is this colored girl *sexy.*

Hammond then set up an important event in jazz history. Seventy-two hours after Bessie Smith cut her last records, under Hammond's auspices and in the same recording studio, Billie Holiday cut her first ones. On November 24, 1933, the indefatigable Hammond had convinced Smith to come up to Manhattan from North Philadelphia for her first recording date in two years. Hammond recalled that she was "virtually penniless and completely depressed.... Bessie was working then at a miserable little gin mill...as a hostess singing pornographic songs for tips." He said:

Holiday, late 1930s. (facing page)

She had given up all hope for a comeback, and was drinking more than ever. I was able to persuade the timid officials at the bankrupt American Columbia company to arrange a session with Bessie for their Okay "race" label. She agreed to come to New York to do the record date, but refused point-blank to record the type of blues that had made her famous. Her argument was that people didn't want to be depressed by blues, they wanted something in a jazz vein.

Benny Goodman and Artie Shaw, c. 1936.

For fifty dollars per number (one-fifth of her salary in her heyday), Smith recorded four songs—"Do Your Duty," "Gimme a Pigfoot," "Take Me for a Buggy Ride," and "Down in the Dumps"—all written in a more-jazz-than-straight-blues idiom by her friends Coot Grant and Sock Wilson. Using a swing-style instrumental group called Buck and His Band, the set included black modernists Chu Berry and Frankie Newton, along with white players Jack Teagarden and (on one side) Benny Goodman. With new songs, new instrumentation, and a voice that was still as strong as a trombone, Smith put together a fine session that represented a bold departure from her classic blues.

For the Holiday session, Hammond—called by some commentators a "militant integrationist"—again used a mixed band, a first for a group called Benny Goodman and His Orchestra. It included Gene Krupa on drums, the Teagarden brothers on trombone and clarinet along with the black players, trumpeter Shirley Clay, and pianist Buck Washington (of the famous team Buck and Bubbles). This was Holiday's first time in a recording studio, and she was visibly nervous. To make matters worse, the cheerless Ethel Waters, who also was recording with Goodman that day, wandered into the studio and stayed around to check out this new "Miss Halliday" in action.

The assembled instrumentalists stood in front of music stands with the parts written out for everybody, including Buck Washington, who, as Holiday knew very well, "couldn't read a note." She was glad Washington was there. Sensing her jumpiness, he leaned down and whispered for her to get herself together.

"You're not going to let these people think you're a square, are you?" he said.

One imagines her glaring at him with curse words on her mind.

"Come on, sing it!" he told her.

It was by no means a great record debut. Krupa's stodgy rhythms boxed in a song already weakened by corny vaudevillian lyrics and a melody line that was not only predictable but also pushed the shrill upper limits of Holiday's range.

Asked about the record in 1957, Holiday put a good face on it: "I get a big bang out of 'My Mother's Son-in-Law.' It sounds like I'm doing *comedy*. (Laughing) My voice sounded so funny and high on there; and I sounded like I'm about three years old. But...I don't like any of my records, to be truthful with you. Because it's always something that you *should* have done. Or you should have waited *here;* or you should have phrased—well, you know how it is." Whatever the record's shortcomings, it inaugurated a new era in jazz singing. What was to follow would not owe as much to Bessie Smith or Louis Armstrong as to the great Billie Holiday.

One slightly better song, "Riffin' the Scotch" (also in 1933, with a Goodman-led studio group) and one fine blues number, "The Saddest Tale" (with Duke Ellington's orchestra, for the extraordinary film *Symphony in Black* in 1935), join "My Mother's Son-in-Law" as works preceding Holiday's great sustained studio work with Teddy Wilson (beginning in July 1935), which many Holiday lovers call her best.

From Monette's, she had suddenly moved to a recording studio. But where had Billie Holiday come from? The myth that Billie Holiday "just grew" was constructed from the stereotype of the Negro natural and the racially gifted. Here in new garb was the American tale of Horatio Alger and his plucky children. According to the myth, what Negroes needed was not skill or practice but a break so they could step boldly forward and get themselves discovered. Is this what happened to spunky young Miss Billie?

No one fed the fires of the Holiday myth machine more than Holiday herself. In 1945, she was interviewed at length by a reporter, Frank Harriott, who wrote for the New York night-scene tabloid *PM*. (Harriott seems to have been the first to conceive the idea of a Billie Holiday book, but it never got off

Holiday at Harlem's Savoy Ballroom, January, 1938. That night Count Basie and Benny Goodman battled to see who was the real king of swing. Holiday, who sang with Basie, looks like a winner. Dave Tough is third from left.

Holiday, 1939, with John Williams and Frankie Newton, leader of both the house band at the Café Society and her first sessions for Commodore Records. (overleaf)

Holiday at age two. Note the flower.
Neither the elaborate dress and shoes
nor the formality of the pose could
keep this toddler from appearing
composed and self-possessed.

Holiday at age sixteen or seventeen,
at the beach. This is one of the only
photographs showing her as a teenager
at leisure. In about a year, she would
begin her recording career.

(facing page)

the ground.) In that interview, she first put out the story that has been repeated so much it seems more believable than the facts. She said she first came north to join her mother, Sadie Fagan, who was a day laborer on Long Island (factually true). She then took her own job in domestic service (there is no evidence of this), but money was tight (easy enough to believe in 1930). Half-truth led to quarter-truth, and then the myth took over completely. She told Harriott:

> After that, I got my first job in show business. I was 14, Mom was sick, and I had to get something that paid a little more money. I went up to Jerry Preston's Log Cabin Club in Harlem and I told them I was a dancer. They gave me an audition, but it didn't turn out. I danced the same step for 15 choruses. They were going to throw me out on my ear, but I kept begging for a job. Finally, the piano player took pity on me. He squashed out his cigarette, looked up at me and said, "Girl, can you sing?" I didn't know what to say. I'd been singing all my life, but never thought I could make any money at it. Anyhow, I told him I could. So I sang "Trav'lin' All Alone." I couldn't believe it, but I had 'em crying in their beer.

She was hired "at $2 a night, six nights a week," and she and Mom were saved.

The one clear note of truth in this statement is that she had been *singing all her life*. Eleanora Fagan, later known to the world as Billie Holiday, was born on April 7, 1915. With her due date coming near, Holiday's mother decided to escape her family's censoring eyes and took a job as a live-in domestic in Philadelphia, trading her services for the assurance that her baby would be born in a hospital, baptized, and properly cared for. This arrangement worked according to plan (though it is not clear whether Sadie's baby was baptized at that time). Contrary to the twice-told tale, Eleanora Fagan was not born in Baltimore but in Philadelphia. Brought back to Baltimore while still an infant, she grew up in that city. Sadie and her daughter moved frequently during the first years of Eleanora's life. Sometimes they moved in with cousins; sometimes they rented a room in a neighbor's home. For two years, they lived on Bond Street in a third-story room in the home of Mrs. Viola Green and her son, Freddie. Freddie Green (not to be confused with Basie's rhythm guitarist of the same name) was a year older than Eleanora and later recalled that she was not exactly obsessed with music. She liked playing pitcher on the sandlot baseball team where she was the only girl, and she liked roller-skating through the streets with her baseball

Holiday and her mother, Sadie Fagan, c. 1944. Holiday signed the nicknames Lester Young first gave them: she was "Duchess," and her mother was "Lady."

buddies. With them, or with some girls she knew, she would scrape together a dime to attend a movie at the Dunbar Theater.

Eleanora was eight or nine years old when, according to her mother, she "used to annoy an aunt with whom she was living by singing…blues about 'my man this and my man that.' Billie was a child, she was told, and had no business singing about such things. But the first song she ever sang was 'My Mammy,' and she used to sing that to me *all* the time!" Green recalls that although nobody paid much attention to it at the time, when Eleanora was twelve or thirteen she liked to listen to Bessie Smith records on his mother's hand-cranked record player. She would sing along with Smith and try to match her tone for tone. "Yeah," he recalled, "I used to hear all those free concerts, Billie Holiday

singing along with Bessie Smith, and I didn't even know what I was listening to.
I'd really like to do that again."

By the mid-twenties, when Eleanora was eleven or twelve, her mother
had moved in with William Hill, whose friends called him "Wee Wee." The
threesome lived at 219 Durham Street, next door to Hill's mother. Interviewed
in 1971, Hill remembered that Eleanora used to sing all the time, throughout
the house. What was she singing in those days? "Whatever songs were around
that time," remembered Hill. "She had a nice voice. Maybe she'd be upstairs
cleaning or in the bathroom." Sometimes, too, she would sing along with the
family radio or record player, both of which he said they had at home. Like many
jazz artists of the twentieth century, including Lester Young and Charlie Parker,
Holiday received an important part of her musical education from records. By
the time she was twelve, she had never left Baltimore but she had heard and
studied closely the leading jazz artists of the world.

For the mythic Billie Holiday, the key sourcebook remains *Lady Sings the
Blues* (1956), the singer's autobiography as stapled together by newspaperman
William Dufty. One of Holiday's long-term pianists of the fifties, Carl Drinkard,
was one of several people close to Holiday who have said that she let Dufty do
the job to get much-needed cash. Despite the publicity shots showing Billie
wearing glasses and typing — two things she never did before or after the photo
session — she did not work on the book herself. She probably never even read it,
Drinkard said. The book portrays her as more of a savvy student of society and
pitiful victim of life than her friends and relatives recalled. For instance, singer
Carmen McRae, who in the 1940s was Holiday's neighbor and friend, told me
in a filmed interview that Holiday's men would hit her but that at times Holiday
was very quick to hit them back. Still, many of the book's exaggerations —
flowing from interviews granted by the singer to reporters over several
decades — do convey a deep emotional truth. They reveal the person Holiday
saw herself to be, her values and sense of life. And when she talked about the
music and the inside world of musicians, she was usually accurate, sometimes
eloquently so.

Relying on the *PM* interview of 1945, Dufty wrote the autobiography's
famous opening lines: "Mom and Pop were just a couple of kids when they
got married. He was eighteen, she was sixteen, and I was three." The truth as
established by official documents, including court records and a passport, runs
counter to these lines. When Eleanora Fagan was born, her mother was nineteen
and her father, Clarence Holiday, seventeen.

Holiday's father, Clarence Holiday. In Baltimore, where he was born, Clarence came to be known as a top banjo and guitar player.

When Holiday arrived in New York about 1930, Clarence was already there. He took her to places where musicians hung out and jammed.

The autobiography's first words manage at once to sensationalize Holiday's beginnings and idealize them. She makes "Pop" somewhat older than "Mom"; she makes them both younger, more innocent, than they would have been when she was three. Most significantly, she imagines that her parents were married. The truth is that they were never married, that they never even lived together.

Leaving aside the tricks of memory and myth indulged in by the highly imaginative Holiday, it *is* true that her father was Clarence Hol(l)iday (at first spelled with two *l*'s and then with one) and that despite his rather casual (some said even callous) sense of his fatherly offices, he exerted a tremendous influence over his daughter.

Born in 1898, Clarence grew up in West Baltimore. By 1914, when he met East Side kid Sadie Fagan, he was an indifferent student at the all-boys high school the kids called the Tin Factory. (The colored high school was a converted plant where tin had been smelted and shaped into cans and boxes.) In the neighborhood surrounding the Tin Factory, Clarence's favorite activities were playing the banjo and talking to pretty girls. He used to wait on the corner to see the girls who went to the Carey Street School, one block around the corner from the Tin Factory. Clarence was a pudgy, affable boy with nut-brown skin, deep-set dark eyes, and a gift of ad lib conversation that won him the nickname of "Lib Lab" among his friends.

More than we generally recognize, Baltimore of the teens and twenties was a music-rich town. There was music in the churches, sometimes involving not just choirs with pianos and organs but church orchestras with harmonicas, trombones, guitars, and drums. Bands worked all over town, playing for occasions of all sorts: there were tent shows and carnivals; church-sponsored picnics and torchlight parades on Friday nights down to the train station or the boat docks; boat and train trips—traveling concerts and dances—to Washington, D.C., or Philadelphia. Pianists worked the movie theaters, improvising tunes and figures to represent the silent still shows' and then the movies' changing frames: "The Night," "True Love," "A Storm." There were street-corner quartets harmonizing minstrel songs and pop tunes of the day, such as "In the Gloaming," "Camptown Races," and "Beautiful Dreamer."

Elmer Snowden, the guitar and banjo player best known for his association with early Duke Ellington units, also attended the Tin Factory and knew Clarence as an excellent player. He recalls seeing Clarence, still in short pants, performing with a group of troubadours, all of whom sang and played banjo. Happy-go-lucky Clarence would be smiling and making eyes at the girls as he went through his act. At fourteen, he was earning tips plus fifty cents a gig, fifty cents more if he worked overtime, and seventy-five cents if he worked out of town.

At night, musicians worked in groups or as solo acts—often for parties in private homes where the piano was the center of attention. At a house party during this period, one might have encountered Baltimoreans Joe Turner, the piano player, or Chick Webb, the drum wizard and bandleader who was later dubbed the "King of the Savoy Ballroom" in New York. Young Duke Ellington and Otto Hardwicke often made the trip from Washington to Baltimore to play and see what the Baltimore musicians were putting down. And, of course, the bands played for public dances—at Mary's Casino on Preston Street or at a big, rough place called Galilee Fishner's Hall in East Baltimore. They also played for the fraternal organizations that sometimes rented Pytheon Castle, homestead of the Knights of Pytheon. Some of them worked the variety houses, burlesque theaters, or small clubs called fast houses or good-time houses where black Baltimoreans came to eat, drink, dance, and, in some cases, pay a dollar extra to spend some time in a room alone with one's own companion or a prostitute. Eubie Blake, Baltimore's premier musician of the time, had gotten his start as a teen playing in saloons and bawdy houses, some of them so rowdy one could barely hear the piano. Baltimore was a port town, where sailors came ashore with brand-new money and an appetite for pleasure. Clarence Holiday grew up knowing the whole scene, from the church altars to the fast houses and what Eubie Blake preferred to call the "hookshops."

Clarence met Sadie after a gig at a carnival. Their romance burned quickly to flame and then, as far as he was concerned, went out. He was still seventeen when Sadie told him she was pregnant with their child. She wanted to get married right away. He was working fairly steadily in the evenings; he could quit school, and they could set up their lives together. She was a pretty, copper-brown eighteen-year-old, short and buxom. She was not a nightlife woman but a warm and witty youngster from a family that worked hard and took pride in its respectability. Her father, Charles, had very light skin (some people took him for white) and worked as a chef in a downtown hotel. Having more money than most blacks in Baltimore, he was a man much admired and, alas, much resented. Sadie was not eager to shock and embarrass him with a "bastard" grandchild.

Sadie herself was born Sara Harris, the illegitimate daughter of Charles Fagan and a woman whose surname was Harris and whose first name is not known. According to Linda Keuhl, "Whoever this woman was, Sadie appears

Ella Fitzgerald and Baltimorean Chick Webb, c. 1938. Fans still debate whether Holiday and Count Basie "outblew" Fitzgerald and Webb at Harlem's Savoy Ballroom in 1937. John Hammond—whose favorite all-time band of all time was Basie's—always said that he was positive Basie was the winner but that Webb's booking agency paid the newspapers to declare in favor of Webb.

The Fletcher Henderson band on the Atlantic City boardwalk, summer 1932. Left to right: Russell Procope, Coleman Hawkins, Edgar Sampson, Clarence Holiday, Walter Johnson, John Kirby, Fletcher Henderson, Russell Smith, Bobby Stark, Rex Stewart, J. C. Higginbotham, and Sandy Williams.

not to have taken her as an ally. Rather, she hitched her star to her father. She adopted his surname and identified with him entirely. She converted to his religion, attended Sunday mass, and kept religious articles in her home." Her stepmother was a woman whose first name began with M — only that letter is legible on Charles's death certificate, to which M bore witness. M was a highly religious Catholic who had converted Charles to her faith and turned up her nose at his Methodist kin, never accompanying him on trips to visit his East Side relatives. M was not at all pleased to have Sadie around the house: why didn't that big girl get herself a job and a place of her own? What Sara Harris, who took for herself the name Sadie Fagan (and who gave her daughter the name Fagan), needed least in the world was the announcement that she had had secret sex with a guitar-plunking playboy who still wore short pants and that now, with no wedding band in sight, she was going to have his baby.

But that was the news. Clarence had just auditioned for a spot in Eubie Blake's band and had been tentatively offered the job. But when Blake found

out that the boy could not read music, the job went to Elmer Snowden instead. Perhaps that is why Clarence began that year to take private lessons with someone named "Toomer," the leader of the group of troubadours with which Clarence was working. Perhaps under the spell of the innovative prejazz giant James Reese Europe—with his highly percussive orchestras of multiple strings—Toomer was teaching Clarence and the other young musicians to play not only banjos and guitars but also mandolins. It was clear to Clarence that if he wanted to hit the big time, he had a lot of work to do. And Sadie? Well, Sadie was all right, but she was just one of the girls. It did excite him that he was going to be a father, though, and as soon as Eleanora was born, he asked Snowden, an old man of fourteen, to be the godfather. Still, he told Sadie that no, he did not want them to get a place together; and no, he wasn't really thinking about getting married.

Clarence Holiday's paternal absenteeism affected Eleanora in very complex, destructive ways. During her early childhood, he was never around except to make rare guest appearances between jobs. Because of this and her

Holiday, early 1930s.

mother's persistent fantasy that they would unite someday as a family, Clarence became a larger-than-life figure. After Eleanora's birth, Sadie, already viewed with suspicion by some of the Fagans, had been firmly rejected by them. Her father's sister, Aunt Rosie, who became the family matriarch, never forgave Sadie and wanted nothing more to do with her or her daughter. Her father was displeased enough to allow his wife to ban Sadie and her child from their home. M had come all the way from a farm in North Carolina to marry this good man and was not about to have things ruined by wide-hipped Sadie, who was acting just like the white folks said colored women acted. So after Sadie returned to Baltimore from Philadelphia, she moved in with her brother John's family and then got full-time work as a maid for a white family on the other side of town. For a while, she rented a house and put a sign out front that read "East Side Restaurant." She did all the cooking and serving herself and, before the place failed, was known as one of the neighborhood's top preparers of soul food and homemade whiskey.

Virtually abandoned by Clarence and cut off by most of her family, Sadie had trouble paying her bills. Still, she tried to make it on her own. She left her brother's home and moved with her daughter from poor neighborhood to poorer neighborhood. Sometimes Charles would slip her some cash, but he had to do so secretly, in order not to incur the wrath of his wife, who was always disgusted at any mention of Sadie (she was not only "common"; she was a reminder of Charles's affair with Ms. Harris) and the horrid granddaughter, Eleanora. In 1920, when Eleanora was five years old, Sadie married a longshoreman named Phil Gough. The marriage seemed to mend the fences with the Fagans; Charles even paid down on a house for his daughter in a fashionable section of West Baltimore. But after three years, Phil Gough disappeared, and Charles took over the house and its payments. Sadie and Eleanora Gough (as Holiday was now generally called) were out of the house and on their own again, with Sadie scrambling to make the rent.

In young Eleanora's mind, Clarence Holiday, with his sporty shirts, flashy banjo and guitar, and "Lib Lab" tales of shows and big-time people in New York, must have seemed enormously powerful and attractive. He was one of the town's underground aristocrats. With money of his own, mobility, and no particular fear that white bosses might lay him off, he was a carefree traveling man. When he *was* around, he did not care much about whether she sat up straight, went to church, or made good grades in school. He had seen her rough-housing with the neighborhood boys and had laughed and called her "Bill." To him, stopping by now and again, she was his own smart little tomboy whether she was her mama's good little girl or not.

Eleanora came to idolize nightlife strongmen: tough guys, often musician-sweetbacks and pimps, from whom she demanded protection and to whom she surrendered a great deal more than just money. These were the "Daddys" she often spoke of in interviews: "I don't know what I'm going to do. Daddy hasn't made our plans yet." "We're going to be together, and we're going to have a home and a baby and contentment." Even as a young teen, she dated fast hustlers whose specialty was not dependable love but control. They shared with her the fantasy of leaping beyond the humdrum middle-class world where even the top earners, like her grandfather, spent their days cooking for white folks. By the time she was fifteen, she had taken as a stage name the one that Clarence had given her, "Billie"—thus having softened the "Bill" and also captured some of the magic associated with film star Billie Dove, whose smooth elegance the Baltimore black girl wanted for herself. When her mother arrived in New York circa 1930, she introduced herself as Sadie Holiday. "And this is my daughter, Eleanora," she would say. "Call me Billie," the teenager would put in, not smiling, determined to look old enough to be part of her father's new and bigger world.

Billie Dove, c. 1930.

As far as music was concerned, Clarence was a positive force for his daughter. He rarely presented his guitar or his banjo as a solo instrument, but he was an outstanding section man, a stomping rhythm string picker and strummer whose accuracy and propulsive sense of the beat's steadiness could swing a whole rhythm section, indeed an entire big band. "Most people don't know it," said Lawrence Lucie, a contemporary of Clarence's who also played outstanding rhythm guitar (and who played on some of the best of the Billie Holiday–Teddy Wilson recording dates), "but the banjo or the guitar is the main instrument in the rhythm section. The drum and the piano can play other things. But the rhythm banjo is the one that holds on to that steady 4/4 beat."

In 1928, Clarence took off with Fletcher Henderson's orchestra, which many considered the most innovative and swinging band in the United States. Since its formation in the early 1920s, Henderson's band had featured Louis Armstrong, Coleman Hawkins, Jimmy Harrison, Don Redman, and Benny Carter—just to name the top stars. Duke Ellington remembered the early Henderson big bands with the highest praise: "Fletcher was a big inspiration to me. His was the band I always wanted mine to sound like when I got ready to have a big band, and that's what we tried to achieve the first chance we had with that many musicians. Obviously, a lot of other musicians wanted the same thing, and when Benny Goodman was ready for a big band, he sent for Fletcher to do his arrangements." Ellington's superlative reed player Harry Carney also recalled the Henderson band's well-earned reputation: "I can remember times when we battled it in its prime and came away defeated." Saxophonist/composer Benny Carter put the case unequivocally: "My goodness, that was the band everybody was hoping to play with! It was the acid test. If you could make it with Fletcher, you could make it with anybody. It was the hardest music and the best music around." Martin Williams has called Henderson's music "an important cultural event in American (and world) history. In one form or another, it reached and moved millions of people, and indeed, helped carry the human spirit through some rather desperate times in the 1930s." Clarence Holiday had guitar-and-banjoed his way to the very summit of the jazz world.

Those who were there to hear the band on gigs have said that Henderson's records do not represent him well. Like Ellington, Henderson was no disciplinarian. Both men figured they should hire the best players in the business, pay them well, and give them great music to play—no lectures or sermons required. Both made the collaborative spirit of jazz music making work toward the creation of a wonderful world of sound. Unlike Ellington, however, Henderson did not make records as if he were a creator of musical history, on fire with the calling to preserve as perfect as possible a legacy of a classic band and its music. Even so, "Sugar Foot Stomp" and "Blue Rhythm" are outstanding Henderson records. They feature work by Bennie Morton (later a regular Billie Holiday sideman) and the great Coleman Hawkins and Rex Stewart—all supported by the supple but steady-dancing guitar beat of Clarence Holiday.

In 1933, for reasons that are not known, Clarence left Henderson and began to float from band to band, often joining forces with Henderson alumni. In 1934, he was with Benny Carter; in 1935, he was with Bob Howard, Charlie Turner, and Louis Metcalf; in 1936, he took his last job, with Don Redman.

One very important point that has not been sufficiently emphasized is that Clarence was something of a singer. He had sung with the troubadours in Baltimore. Fanny Holiday, whom Clarence married in 1924, remembered that Clarence used to romance her at home with his singing. And Walter Johnson, Clarence's colleague in the Henderson band, recalled Clarence's singing in relation to his daughter Billie's: "He was very proud of her. But he was a good singer himself. Oh yes. He used to sing with the band. He'd sing a lot of sweet songs, ballads, no blues or nothing like that. 'Million Dollar Baby'—I remember he used to do an arrangement on that. I never heard anybody sing that like he sang it. A style kind of like her. Not exactly, but something like her style." Fanny Holiday also reported that Clarence even convinced Henderson to let Billie sing with the Henderson band on occasion. The band's trombonist, Sandy Williams, remembered that Holiday and Henderson were on the same bill in Chicago in 1936, with the band backing her up. According to Fanny, Clarence wanted Henderson to take his daughter as the band's regular "girl singer," but for reasons that were never clear (Fanny always thought it was to avoid family tensions within the band), Henderson said no. In any case, both Holidays were singers, and — if Fanny's memory is to be credited — as instrumentalist and singer, the two had a chance to perform together.

In terms of musical influence, Billie was probably most turned on by her father's easy-seeming and yet complexly accurate sense of time. If Bobby Tucker and others said Holiday's time was as perfect as a metronome's (more so, since no metronome could accent or style the beat as Holiday could), perhaps it is because from the beginning of her conscious life, she was aware that her father's job was that of the perfect jazz band's perfect timekeeper. He was what Benny Green called, in another context, the "clock that laughs," the man who smiled as he nonchalantly swung the band by keeping time much better than a clock.

Her father was not just any jazz musician; he was an obvious success. Here it was the Depression and a nadir period for black-white relations, and Lib Lab was a top pro. He had freedom of movement, personal stylishness, ease of artistic expression, the respect of fellow musicians and music lovers alike, and flashy clothes and cash in his pocket — all of which went with being a regular member of the top jazz orchestra.

With Clarence's example in mind, sometime in the mid-1920s, well before she was singing professionally, Eleanora, obviously "one of those supersubtle fry," a whiz kid "upon whom nothing was lost," began to give up on the middle-class world her mother represented — the world of church, school, and hard work at menial jobs.

In the newspaper *PM* (William Dufty's key source for the stories in *Lady Sings the Blues*), Holiday recalled that when she was six or seven, she was left with cruelly pious Cousin Ida, who beat her every day. This Ida, Holiday said, would hit her with a whip or with her fists, charging her with wetting the bed, a crime, according to Holiday, that her cousin Henry (Ida's son) was guilty of. But Ida was sure Eleanora was the bad one, just like her mother. In *Lady Sings the Blues,* Holiday says of her aunt :

She never got through telling my mother I was going to bring home a baby and disgrace the damn family like she did. One time she heard me say "Damn it" and she thought this was so sinful she tossed a pot of hot starch at me. She missed, though, because I ducked. You couldn't tell her nothing about Henry, why that boy used to give us girls [cousin Eleanora and his sister, Elsie] a terrible time. He even tried to do what we called "that thing" to us while we were sleeping. Sometimes we would be so tired from fighting this little angel off all night, we wouldn't wake up in time for school.

But the worst was yet to come. Holiday tells of a ninety-six-year-old great-grandmother whom she adored. "The old lady used to tell me how it felt to be a slave, to be owned body and soul by a white man who was the father of her children. She couldn't read or write, but she knew the Bible by heart from beginning to end and she was always ready to tell me a story from the Scriptures." Eleanora was six and did not know Great-Grandmother had orders from her doctor never to sleep lying down but sitting up in a chair. The old woman implored Eleanora to let her lie down beside her, so Eleanora helped her stretch out on the floor, where the young girl fell asleep to the murmur of the old woman's bedtime story. "I woke up four or five hours later. Grandma's arm was still tight around my neck and I couldn't move it. I tried and tried and then I got scared. She was dead, and I began to scream…. They had to break Grandma's arm to get me loose." After a month in the hospital recovering from what was diagnosed as shock, Eleanora came home to the wrath of Cousin Ida, who "started right in where she had left off, beating me."

What is most interesting in Holiday's recollection of events, which no interviews or other documents substantiate, is her presentation of herself and her plight. Abandoned by her parents, she was subjected to sexual mistreatment at the place she was expected to call home. She was served an unending round of punishments by her surrogate mother, and her attempt to embrace the family matriarch — the great-grandmother, who was illiterate but fully schooled in the Bible and tested by the hellfires of slavery — led to the old woman's destruction and thus to a death lock of guilt, shock, and continued corporal punishment for

East Baltimore, c. 1920.

Holiday. It is not surprising that this youngster, who was not exactly pious but who did attend church as often as her mother could make her go, figured that she was to blame for having been set adrift in an uncaring world. Doubtless part of the answer to questions of Holiday's later preference for circumstances and men who would control and punish her is to be found in her painful beginnings. She knew in her heart that she had not been the nice little girl that Sadie Fagan had meant her to be.

For the historian in search of reliable sources concerning Holiday, the trail is a stark one: no birth certificate, no infant baptismal record, no listing in the city directory. The written record of her existence begins with her first arrest. She was ten years old. Because her mother had to fill out forms, we learn that she was born in Philadelphia, not Baltimore (as Billie knew but would never acknowledge). Holiday's own account of that first arrest appears in *Lady Sings the Blues*. Presumably, she told William Dufty that her mother was still in town but out of the house for a moment when a neighbor named Mr. Dick lured her to another neighbor's place on the pretext that Sadie had asked him to take her there. The place turned out to be a house of prostitution, where, with the aid of the madam, he raped her. When Sadie brought the officials to the scene, somehow Eleanora was held responsible:

> *They treated me like I'd killed somebody. They wouldn't let my mother take me home. Mr. Dick was in his forties and I was only ten. Maybe the police sergeant took one look at my breasts and limbs and figured my age from that. I don't know. Anyway, I guess they had me figured for having enticed this old goat into the whorehouse or something. All I know for sure is they threw me into a cell. My mother cried and screamed and pleaded, but they just put her out of the jail house and turned me over to a fat white matron. When she saw I was still bleeding, she felt sorry for me and gave me a couple of glasses of milk. But nobody else did anything for me except give me filthy dirty looks 'and snicker to themselves.*

Mr. Dick, Holiday says, was sentenced to five years in prison. "They sentenced me to a Catholic institution." Again, what Holiday reports is grotesquely betrayed trust, sexual violence, and outrageous and undeserved punishments. It is a tale of institutional failure: the family, the neighborhood as an extended family, the law all failed her, pronouncing her guilty for her predicament.

As easy as it is to believe that Eleanora was raped and blamed for it—and that she and her mother were powerless to obtain justice—the documents pertaining to that first arrest tell a different tale. Court records show that the fourth-grader was on the hook from school so often that a probation officer named M. Dawson took her to juvenile court, where, in January 1925, Magistrate Williams declared her guilty of being "a minor without proper care and guardianship" and ordered her to spend a year in Baltimore's Catholic-run House of the Good Shepherd for Colored Girls.

Back to Holiday's version of what happened: She recalls that once at the House of the Good Shepherd, she enjoyed a degree of fame among the inmates because she was there for a sex crime. The worst of it, she says, was that once the sisters running the place punished her for breaking the rules by making her distribute to the other girls a basketful of food sent by her mother. Then they locked her in a room with one of the girls who had died. Was it the girl who had broken the rule against swinging too high on the playground and broken her neck ("God will punish her. God will punish her," the mother superior had told the gawking onlookers)? For rule tester Eleanora, the experience was horrific: "All I knew was I couldn't stand dead people ever since my great-grandmother

The singer Mildred Bailey, c. 1940. She hired Holiday's mother as her maid, and then needled Holiday about how poor a cook and housekeeper Sadie was. "This," according to John Hammond, "was Mildred's way of getting back at Holiday because Holiday was so good."

Holiday's baptismal certificate, 1925. The priest who baptized her at the House of the Good Shepherd checked with Billie's mother, Sadie—"Sara Harris (Mrs. Sara Gough)"—and then described Billie's circumstances, in Latin, as follows: "Natural child. Born in hospital. In Philadelphia. And (according to her mother) baptized in the same place. I cannot obtain any record of the baptism and today I baptized her and absolved her, conditionally."

had died holding me in her arms. I couldn't sleep. I couldn't stand it. I screamed and banged on the door so, I kept the whole joint from sleeping. I hammered on the door until my hands were bloody." Looking back on the scene and the consequences of her first arrest, Holiday again conjured up images of failed communication with family, punishments that were excruciatingly painful, both physically and metaphysically (by confinement with the dead), and guilt.

Mary "Pony" Kane, who also did time at Good Shepherd, has confirmed that it was a place of strict routines and terrible, swift punishments. She added that most of the girls were thirteen to eighteen years old, many of them long-termers who were very tough. Frequently, a new girl's initiation involved having sex, willingly or unwillingly, with one of the veteran inmates. Kane confirmed, too, that nine- to ten-year-old Eleanora, with her gorgeous face and prematurely shapely figure, would have been quite vulnerable to such attacks. To survive the sisters, she would have to obey to the letter the Good Shepherd's unbending rules; to survive the inmates, she would have to learn to fight them and probably trade with them not just candy but sexual favors as well.

One of the women who worked at the House of the Good Shepherd, Christine Scott, was eighty-four when she talked with an interviewer about young Eleanora. Correctly remembering that Eleanora was called Madge (not Theresa, as Holiday says in *Lady Sings the Blues*) at the Good Shepherd, Scott recalled the ten-year-old not as a street-smart sharpie but as an older-looking "child" who was painfully introverted and shy:

> *Madge [Eleanora] was nothing but a child. But she was quite plump and tall as any fourteen-year-old girl. Very nice looking brown skin. Her features was even and light…and she had a nice suite of hair. Nice and clean was she. But I tell you she was just almost like a stick. Took no interest in anything but sewing. Always down in the dumps. Very seldom had anything to do with nobody else. In the classroom, she would go sit by herself. And when she went out into the yard, she would go to sit alone.*

Scott remembered that more than anything, Eleanora wanted to be baptized. With Scott standing in as her godmother, the House of the Good Shepherd priest, Father Edward V. Casserly, performed the baptism on March 19, 1925. Scott recalled:

> *She was in there with the rest of the girls, all of them in white dresses and veils. She was grinning from ear to ear. You could almost see her back teeth. She was just as light as a feather. The sisters gave her Mary rosary beads. She was so tickled. Oh, and yes, I give her a prayer book. I almost forgot that. She must've appreciated it 'cause she always kept it in her hand. After that she used to come from dinner and sit down right on the floor beside me. We didn't talk much. She was a right good girl.*

Back home, things had changed. Her mother was about to move out of her apartment and into a house on Durham Street with Wee Wee Hill. It was to this place on Durham that Eleanora returned. This was the house where Hill remembered teenage Eleanora walking through the rooms singing. For a while, the scene was stable; there was good reason to sing.

But Hill and Fagan began to disagree. Hill was a dependable porter at the B & O Building in downtown Baltimore, but, eight years younger than Sadie, he liked to flirt with other women and to stay out late partying. "I guess I was a bad fella," he later recalled. One night Sadie could not find Hill and tracked him to a brothel on Bond Street. He was upstairs when he heard a loud rapping on the front door—quite unusual for these secret places. In a very loud voice, Sadie began to call his name and demand that he come outside and answer to her. "When I knew who it was, I didn't come out then, naturally," Hill said. No one unlocked the front door. Twelve-year-old Eleanora was at home with her mother when Hill returned later that evening. As Hill told it, there was confusion: "When I came home, she grabbed a wooden cigarette stand with prongs and she swung it and cut my wrist and arm. And she was cussing me, but I wouldn't fight her. I ran. I wanted to get away. Eleanora tried to stop her, tried to talk to her. So I didn't stay with her. So I went to my mother's. Then I came back. We didn't have any other fight like that. That's the only time she ever hurt me…. It surprised me. At the time it did. Because I didn't think she would care that much to hurt me."

Things fell apart. But before the end of the affair, which lasted about four years, Sadie received her divorce from Phil Gough and began pressing Hill to marry her. She put together a plan to improve the trio's economic picture. It was a New York plan that would eventually give Eleanora a series of "breaks" (not only a set of opportunities but also a traumatizing round of disruptions). Sadie and Hill moved to Cedarhurst, Long Island, and took jobs with a Jewish family named Levy. Sadie was the Levys' cook and maid, while Hill worked as a porter in their store in Times Square.

There are conflicting reports about where Eleanora stayed in Baltimore after Sadie and Hill took off for New York. Mary "Pony" Kane said that Eleanora moved into the household of Hill's mother, Miss Lucy Hill, called "Miss Lu." As Hill told it, he gave Eleanora enough money to pay for a room and board near Pratt and Gough streets. Maybe both arrangements were tried. In either case, the youngster found herself with more freedom than she had ever had before. Miss Lu had injured her leg, which was never properly set, so she just stayed indoors lying on a hospital bed or sitting with her leg propped up on a box set on the parlor floor. Miss Lu had family members and renters coming and going: her son Wee Wee and Sadie Fagan, Wee Wee's two brothers, one brother's wife, and probably sometimes Eleanora. To help with the work, Pony Kane, then a teenager, moved into Miss Lu's attic with her mother. All shared the close quarters at 217 Durham Street, a simple old house with a "summer kitchen," according to Kane, and a no-good bath at the rear.

Kane recalled this as a dark gaslit house where many people came and went. All day and all night, doors were opening and closing, out back and out front, and people were always stepping quietly up the stairs. Miss Lu had promised Sadie that she would take care of Eleanora, and she tried to be true to her word. But Eleanora had spent a year in reform school and was an admirer of the night-town world of her father. She ran rings around her guardian, agreeing to be a good girl and then taking off for hours. No question about it, Eleanora knew just what it meant to be respectful and well mannered in the southern black tradition; she could turn on the good behavior if her mother were down for the weekend or she wanted something. But beginning in the first weeks that her mother was away, she began to skip school regularly and to explore in detail the parts of East Baltimore where nobody went out to school or work and everybody had extra cash and dressed to kill.

"Eleanora was getting around fast," recalled Kane, who already had been hustling in Baltimore's red-light district of the 1920s. "You know the kind of people that say, 'I'm going to get cussed out anyways, so what's the difference? What the hell?' Well, Eleanora went out and done what she felt like doing 'cause she was just *don't-carish.*"

In those days, Eleanora was a tacky dresser, wearing odd colors and fuzzy sweaters. "She'd get a pair of stockings," Kane said, "wash 'em out, and put 'em on half dry, and go out. She didn't have too much clothes or nothing." And she remembered seeing Eleanora creeping past Miss Lu, long after midnight, with her face away from the light so the old lady would not see the heavy makeup she was wearing to hide her swollen and cut-up face. "She liked the fellas that dressed nice," Kane said. "Nob shoes with wing toes…leather, different colors: brown, black, and like a wine color. They used to wear pinstripe gray, the best-dressed fellas. With caps on and the caps used to come from Matteburgs…what the hustlers wore." Some of the men Eleanora liked worked regular jobs, but eventually she had no time for working squares and spent all of her time with hustlers and pimps.

There can be no question that Eleanora's "don't-carish" behavior was motivated by adolescent mischief as well as the thrill of defying the social hierarchy by identifying not with the school or church kids but with the underworld aristocracy of nightlife hustlers. Nor can we doubt that she felt she was taking a fantastic step into the dark world of her prince of a father, the after-hours world that viewed the realm enforced upon her—the realm of school, church, and petty politeness—with caution and contempt. Yes, she was

Billie Holiday's Baltimore, c. 1930.

trading one way of life for another, at least tentatively. She also was trading one idea of a family for another: the night world offered a sure and changeless code of insiders' rules. Pimp/boyfriends were "daddies"; older street women were protective, initiating "mamas"; and there were "brothers" and "sisters" of all sorts. Here at least was a family that was not always packing up to leave her behind with people she knew did not care much about her.

Eleanora was twelve years old when she befriended the tough and street-smart Ethel Moore, who owned the house at 20 Bond Street in Fell's Point, Baltimore's waterfront red-light district. Insiders called it the Point. Moore's place was not a bordello but a good-time house—an all-night party place where black Baltimoreans came not to buy sex specifically, but to dance, drink, smoke reefer, and perhaps rent a room for an hour or so. Moore helped teach Eleanora the rules of the Point, including the tricks of the prostitution trade (*trade* was their word for sex with a John). Moore served as a hip guide and protector, and even something of a big sister, to this young girl at odds with her own family.

Alice Dean ran a flourishing Fell's Point bordello and clip joint, where it was standard procedure, according to one former prostitute, to take a John's wallet while he was trading with another girl who later shared the cash. Like Moore, Dean took Eleanora just as she was, exposing her to a new way of life that spelled glittering elegance, fast money of her own, and at least as clear a code of behavior as the straight world could boast. Pimps like Skinny "Rim" Davenport played the role of Big Daddy, keeping their ladies in line with offers of love (obviously shared) and with disciplinary actions that were regular, quick, and violent. What Holiday said about her days as a prostitute in New York was also true of trading in Baltimore: it meant "regular white customers" (blacks generally could not afford Dean's) and "it was a cinch. They had wives and kids to go home to. When they came to see me it was wham, bang, they gave me the money and were gone." Here at best was a part-time lover whom she did not expect to depend on, or at worst a stupid white man to trick, rob, and laugh at later.

In her autobiography, Holiday reports working at Dean's house, but not as a call girl. As usual, she airbrushes the early portrait of herself, giving her age not as ten but as sixteen. At sixteen, she says, she was full-grown, "a woman.... I was big for my age, with big breasts, big bones, a big fat healthy broad, that's all." Even so, like the plucky Horatio Alger hero that she portrays herself to be, she "started working out then, before school and after, minding babies, running errands, and scrubbing those damn white steps all over Baltimore. When families in the neighborhood used to pay me a nickel for scrubbing them down, I decided

I had to have more money, so I figured out a way. I bought me a brush of my own, a bucket, some rags, some Octagon soap, and a big white bar of that stuff I can't ever forget—Bon Ami."

Alice Dean's, she says, was just one of the places where she earned change for doing chores: "I used to run errands for her and the girls. I was very commercial in those days. I'd never go to the store for anybody for less than a nickel or a dime. But I'd run all over for Alice and the girls, and I'd wash basins, put out the Lifebuoy soap and towels."

What *is* believable is that Eleanora was drawn into more and more daring ventures inside black Baltimore's hustling scene. For our purposes, what is most significant about that secret world is that whatever else it was—and surely it was a world where the hustling man was as "gracile and dangerous as a tiger"—it also was a world of elegance and exceedingly fine music. Holiday later said that she ran errands for Dean in exchange for the chance to hang around her front parlor and hear Bessie Smith on the Victrola. "If I'd heard Louis and Bessie at a Girl Scout jamboree," Holiday says defensively, "I'd have loved it just the same. And in Baltimore, places like Alice Dean's were the only joints fancy enough to have a Victrola and for real enough to pick up on the best records."

No one in Baltimore seems to remember Eleanora scrubbing steps or running errands for anybody. What some do recall is that twelve-year-old Eleanora looked significantly older than her years and that she was regularly brought along to fast houses as well as to Alice Dean's and other out-and-out bordellos. Pony Kane recalled Alice Dean's quite vividly:

> *She had everything in that house. She had a beautiful house. She had a graphophone. You know, you used to wind it up and you put a record on. They used to sing and dance to death. They played the "Black Bottom" and "Stormy Weather." And a whole lot of blues they used to sing—Blue Suzy stuff, Butter Beans and Suzy stuff. They had all of Florence Mills's records, Bessie Smith and Mamie Smith. They were mostly with them blues singers. Them women, they used to snap their fingers. Especially on Mondays. Yeah, Monday was Blue Monday.*

Kane also recalled seeing Eleanora at Dean's: "She was the youngest of all the girls. She used to wear satin slips and panties. Her being young, different fellas would like her." Before long, she was steadily in demand at Dean's—a favorite

In her autobiography, Holiday claims to have earned money scrubbing Baltimore's famed white steps. But friends who knew her have denied it, saying that she worked in private clubs as a fledgling singer and sometimes as a prostitute.

FLASH

WEEKLY NEWSPICTURE MAGAZINE

10¢

MAY 3, 1937

"pretty baby" of the paying customers. "And all the women were jealous of her," Kane said, "because she was light-complected, and well-built, and she could sing."

Recall that these were places not just of sex but also of music. Customers would request the young girl who sang just for them. And when, for the whole place to hear, she did her special number of singing along with phonograph records in her smoky Bessie- and Louis-like voice, the whole house would be rocking.

In those days, a weekday evening might start with a house party. Manager "Diesel" Haskins, who knew Eleanora in those early days in Baltimore, set the scene: "You take two or three piano players with us to somebody's house where they have a piano. And the parents sit around and listen, and then go to bed, and we just play into the early morning, singing, dancing. And then we go home and wash up and change to go to school. Billie sang 'Sentimental Baby' and 'Teardrops.'" While others quit for the night, Eleanora and her faster crowd would head for small clubs in East Baltimore. Skinny Davenport recalled that Eleanora "used to sing every night." He said: "First she would sing at the place on Bethel and Pratt, and then she would come up on Central and Pratt, and then she would go up here on Baltimore and Dallas. Different nights she'd be at different places and then we'd follow her."

On nights when she had no prearranged gig, Eleanora would sometimes join forces with other girl singers to see if they could stir up a chance to sing for tips. One friend named Ethel Young and another named Eva "Nitey" Beasley would get together in this way, singing from club to club. On Amateur Night at the old Custer Theater, the girls would pile in and try to get turns onstage, to see "who had the most lyrics" and who could claim the most applause.

When everything else shut down for the night, at about two or three in the morning, Eleanora's crowd would take off for Ethel Moore's place or to another of the after-hours good-time houses. Davenport said that he and the other night men had particular regard for Eleanora. She was young, but she was a smart conversationalist. She was talented and sharp looking, she knew how to fight, and she was not scared of anybody. And she was beginning—as a performer and a streetwise hustler—to have some money of her own. "At that time," Davenport said, "a place could stay open as long as they want. The clubs would close up…and then Eleanora would go to the after-hours house like Ethel's place. We'd be partying together, and she would sing a song if we'd ask her. We didn't have no piano. She would just sing. Or like we'd put a record on that had no words to it, and she would sing the words." Davenport and his boys, along with Nitey Beasley and other members of the all-night team, would drink bootleg whiskey, smoke joints, eat fish and ribs, and dance to the music of the jukebox, the piano, or Eleanora—and sometimes all three together. And as Fats Waller put it, *"Here 'tis, the joint was jumping!"*

Alice Dean's and Ethel Moore's, whose sociology and ethics could bear little scrutiny, were fertile training grounds for jazz musicians. American jazz, the most democratic of art forms, was nurtured in saloons, up-the-backstairs whorehouses, and good-time joints—places with no official sanctions or sanctioners; places where having a good voice or a proper song meant nothing compared to being able to swing in the rhythm of the places themselves and to make them swing; places free of the thou-shalt-nots of the culture at large and therefore free for performers to try new things, to invent, to be pioneering workers along the frontiers of a new music. Billie Holiday's music started in places where people came not to hear a concert, but to enjoy singing that, at its best, was part and parcel of the dancing, the revelry, the flirting, the lovemaking —the bawdy and yet somehow elegant rituals of conjuring up good times and deflecting the bad.

Those who frequented these places had very high musical standards. Out of them emerged the likes of Eubie Blake, Elmer Snowden, and Clarence and Billie Holiday. Just as her father had done a few years before, Eleanora encountered local stars and out-of-town musicians such as Duke Ellington and Gertie Wells, two of Washington's top piano players. She also saw some of the not-so-famous Baltimoreans who never left town and never made a record but who knew their craft inside and out. In these intimate places, where artistic standards were high and the give-and-take between musician and musician and between musician and dancer and audience was expected and indeed required, Eleanora Fagan, singer, flourished.

By 1929 or 1930, when it seems Miss Lu contacted Sadie Fagan in New York and told her that Eleanora was out of control, fourteen- or fifteen-year-old Billie was more than just plain "don't-carish." She held the straight world in contempt, but she had something of her own to care about: the music.

"No camera," one writer said, "could ever contrive to capture once and for all the elusive essence of Billie Holiday…[seven] pictures taken in her twenties and thirties are so strikingly dissimilar that they might pass for portraits of seven different women." She could appear soft and elegantly lovely; buxom and busting loose with country cuteness; fat and tomboyish; thin, angular, and aloofly svelte; puffy faced and arch, the Lady of long evenings and deep cynicism; open and friendly at cigarette-break time, glad to see you; the contrived Lady Day, posing in fur, jewelry, and a silver dress. They were all her, and there were many other faces as well. No wonder top photographers such as Roy De Carava, Carl Van Vechten, and Robin Carson sought her out. They all took wonderful Holiday shots. There were so many Billies to shoot for.

Her many names reflect some of these many roles. She was born Eleanora Fagan, but her father called her "Bill"; then she was Eleanora Gough when her mother married Phil Gough and then Eleanora Fagan again when her mother was divorced; at the House of the Good Shepherd, she was given the name "Madge" (in her book she remembers it as "Theresa") not just to protect her real identity but to signal that she must renounce her old ways and start over as a new person; back home she was Eleanora Fagan once again; she became Billie Holliday and then Billie Holiday (and for a brief period, so she would not be seen only as Clarence's daughter, she was Billie Halliday); Count Basie, whose name also was Bill, called her "William" (sometimes when she was in session with a group of women she knew well or she wanted to signal a sexual interest in another woman, she would announce that her name was William); "Lady Day" was Lester Young's name for her (Carmen McRae said that he first gave the title to her mother, Sadie, but that Billie, whom Lester had at first dubbed the "Dutchess," preferred Lady and just took it); starting in the forties, many people who were close to her just called her Lady; and then, to top it all off, the French sometimes referred to her as "La Holiday." She also had several married names, some of them representing fake marriages: Eleanora or Billie Monroe and McKay were true married names. Eleanora or Billie Guy, Levy, and others represented either wishful thinking or a disguise to fool the public. When she was brought into Metropolitan Hospital with her last illness, she was registered as Eleanora McKay.

All of this naming and unnaming — reclaiming the maternal or the paternal name, borrowing the name of a starlet, titling oneself, using one name as a badge of opportunity and another as a disguise — is an American tradition. American studies scholar Joseph W. Reed puts the case succinctly: "There is in Americans (along with the ambivalence) the love of disguise or mask. The mask we like best is the poker player's bluff, impassive for good reason and for profit, not for the sake of distance or imperiousness. 'When you call me that, *smile*,' says Owen Wister's Virginian. We want to get something out of getting dressed up." Ralph Ellison, whose characters in both fiction and nonfiction are expert role players, calls America "a land of masking jokers. We wear the mask for purposes of aggression as well as for defense; when we are projecting the future and preserving the past. In short, the motives hidden behind the mask are as numerous as the ambiguities the mask conceals." And it was Yeats, with Ellison as his witness, who observed that "if we cannot imagine ourselves as different from what we are and assume the second self, we cannot impose a discipline upon ourselves, though we may accept one from others. Active virtue, as distinct from the passive acceptance of a current code, is the wearing of a mask." Nothing masks one quite so well as a new name. How many Americans arrive at a new home — whether in the New World or in a new town, city, or region — and take for themselves a new name and thus a new identity with which to face, or avoid facing, the world?

Certainly African American history, from African kingdoms to slave ships and from slavery toward freedom, has brought many a thousand changes of name. One of the first errands of many black slaves who became free was to assert what Booker T. Washington called their "entitles": they threw off the names given them by their former owners and gave themselves names that had in them the ringing sound of freedom. It is significant that in the choice of the name Billie Holiday and even Lady Day (a royalized then shortened version of Holi-Day) was a break with the past, represented by the name Fagan, with its negative Baltimore connections and its linkage to a slave and even a shadowy Irish past. What Ellison says of black writers and would-be writers also is true of the sensitive Billie Holiday:

> *And when we are reminded so constantly that we bear, as Negroes, names originally possessed by those who owned our enslaved grandparents, we are apt, especially if we are potential writers, to be more than ordinarily concerned with the veiled and mysterious events, the fusions of blood, the furtive couplings, the business transactions, the violations of faith and loyalty, the assaults; yes, and the unrecognized and recognizable loves through which our names were handed down to us.*

The choice of the name Billie Holiday represented not just a rejection of her history but a celebration as well. What she kept was her favorite part of the past—the Hollywood-hopeful part, the free spirit, the tomboy who was connected with her father, the Billie. She explicitly retained the Holiday because she wanted to be known as her daddy's daughter; she was a musician, too, or would be in time. As a namer, she was not only revising the past but also looking to the future. No doubt she also liked the music of the new name and the suggestion that this Miss Billie was on permanent vacation: she was Billie *Holiday*. (This suggestion in her name must have felt painfully ironic in the late forties and fifties, when her need for drugs and the slave-driving of her men made taking even one night off exceedingly difficult.)

Lady Day also has a mellifluous sound to it. One imagines that she liked the idea that Lady means good etiquette, as well as the authority to decide exactly what good etiquette means, and that it suggests high style and mythic responsibilities. This lady of the night world was also the daunting Lady of *Day*. Inevitably, Lady Day also reminded her of her father's world and her connection with other "royal" persons there: Duke Ellington, Earl Hines, Count Basie, and

Holiday, mid 1940s.

under her dubbing (as she explains, it was given when Roosevelt was president and the title meant something grand), President Lester Young, the "Prez." Our names, Ellison says, "become our masks and our shields and the containers of all those values and traditions which we learn and/or imagine as being the meaning of our familial past." With her names, Holiday staked her claim to part of her blood history and improvised a title of kinship in the Royal House of Jazz: *"Lady Day" to you.*

If Billie Holiday photographed or even named was a tricky business, the numerous efforts to capture her on paper, on film, or in stage accounts have been equally problematic. Like Brer Fox, she concealed her own face and placed in the pathway of those who would describe her a sticky tar baby in her image. She lied to interviewers. She made up a childhood and married parents. She told whoppers about how she started singing, which songs she wrote, and how she wrote them. Hers was a story for hire. She sold preposterous versions of it, written by hacks, to *Ebony* magazine and its affiliates *Tan* and *Jet*. *Ebony* wanted one of its writers to do her autobiography with her, and at first she was willing.

But somehow the deal fell through. The agreement to let William Dufty tell her story sprang from his steadfastness, casual demeanor, and professionalism. He got her a fat advance up front and drew up a contract that was clear and fair. She also liked him right away and appreciated the fact that he did not expect her to dictate the thing to him. He would look up her story and then use the anecdotes she gave him in her helter-skelter conversational style to flesh it out. She also must have liked him for not cross-examining her on her various versions of past events. It was Dufty's view that no long library checking was required: this was *her* story (even if she was making it up), and as long as no laws were broken, her telling of it was at least as valid as anyone else's.

For her it was a straightforward matter of quick cash and publicity. Whether she worked on it much or even read it over, it stands as the key sourcebook for the Holiday myth. All other accounts spring from this presentation of Holiday as a "hep kitty" gone wrong, a brilliant victim of drugs and draggy circumstance. What I find missing in the Dufty account, and in all of the other prose narratives, plays, and movies that retell her life, is the careful

exploration of her role as an artist. She was the greatest jazz singer of all time. With Louis Armstrong, she invented modern jazz singing. Why do these accounts, which tell us so much about her drug problems, no-good men, and supposedly autobiographical sad songs, tell us so little about Billie Holiday, artist?

The answer is that aside from racism, sexism, and confusion about what art and artists are all about, Holiday herself was an extremely complex woman. People who knew her well—several of whom were close enough to see her alone for hours at a time and even live in her house—have said that at age forty, she was at once tough as nails and weak as a small child; strong and quick to fight you, yet strangely fragile and vulnerable, desperate for protection; haughty and brusque, yet haunted by an inferiority complex; arrogant and controlling of others, yet arrogantly controlled by her pimp/husband/managers; a bisexual who bragged about her "girls," even claiming at times to have been a pimp who would rough up her "chicks"; a frustrated housewife who loved to cook for "Daddy" and wanted to quit singing, settle down, and have a baby of her own. The truth seems to be that she was all of these things. Some of them, such as the tyrannized woman who became an abuser of women and the arrogant woman with an inferiority complex, are not at all surprising.

What none of these dualities tell us much about is her artistry. At the very least, art gave order to a world greatly threatened by entropy and violence. Apropos here is Stanley Crouch's point that jazz is phenomenal in its capacity to give form to experience not just of the past but of that most confusing of times, the present. It should be noted that in Holiday's Baltimore community of the teens and twenties, it was not easy to find a place where a woman of color was free to do more professionally than clean houses and clothes or sell her body. Music offered one such place. As her father's example showed, that road was possible. Even though the jazz band was an almost exclusive male club of freedmen, the example of the blues divas of the period showed a way out for women, too. And the jazz life suggested a way of reconstructing or revising the past, of reclaiming her father by joining his traveling family of music makers.

•   •   •

As a singer, Billie Holiday had three distinct periods. Most commentators falter on this point. Knowing or preferring only one or two of the three Holiday styles, they diminish the others or dismiss them outright. The typical outline for a discussion of Holiday's career is as follows: (1) the great stuff of the thirties,

Holiday, c. 1948. (facing page)

"out of nowhere"; (2) "Strange Fruit" and the beginning of the decline; (3) the final years, when she miserably imitated herself. I see quite a different Holiday career chart, in which the three Holidays have equal stature: richly innovative in the thirties; just as creative in the forties; equally so in the fifties. That is not to say that there were no valleys and only peaks. But there is brilliant material from all three periods, along with some clunkers. Even as her voice deepened and darkened with the hard late years, her singing grew more profound. While I love the voice of Holiday as a teenager and a woman in her early twenties, I agree with Martin Williams that the Holiday of the 1950s was not only a more

compelling dramatic performer, but also an even greater jazz singer because she was a better musician. I describe the first Holiday in this chapter, then turn to the other two in Part IV.

•   •   •

The first Billie Holiday is the one we have heard the most about so far. This was the girl of sixteen whom Bobby Henderson met, the one who had been nurtured in Baltimore's dark houses, where she sang along with the Victrola or with piano accompaniment in her now bell-clear, now intimately husky style.

Back in Baltimore, she was present during "musicians' battles," when two or more bands would play against each other to see which one the crowd preferred. She could see that for the musicians, these contests were not just to please a crowd; at their best, they were sessions where musicians "took one another to school," where those who were tough enough to endure all the pressures involved—including at times the pressing situation in which someone who sat in and outplayed you might claim your chair in what used to be your band—could learn quite a lot as they put together artistic identities of their own.

In jam sessions, individual players educated each other in the same confrontational way. Elmer Snowden recalled, "To find out who was the best piano player or banjo player, each man would put up five dollars. One would play, then the other, and you'd settle by applause." Ralph Ellison has described jam sessions as intense ritual affairs that could be every bit as demanding as a classical player's conservatory experience:

> *Here it is more meaningful to speak, not of courses of study, of grades and degrees, but of apprenticeship, ordeals, initiation ceremonies, of rebirth. For after the jazzman has learned the fundamentals of his instrument and the traditional techniques of jazz — the intonations, the mute work, manipulation of timbre, the body of traditional styles — he must then "find himself," must be reborn, must find, as it were, his soul. All this through achieving that subtle identification between his instrument and his deepest drives which will allow him to express his own unique ideas and his own unique voice. He must achieve, in short, his self-determined identity.*

In Baltimore, Holiday would join jam sessions and try her best to "outblow" other singers and instrumentalists. Even before she came to New York, it would have been obvious to her — though she never would have expressed it as Ellison did — that in jam sessions, she was seeking to achieve the "self-determined identity" about which he writes and that, as he says, she sought her "soul."

Ellison also has written that "true jazz is an art of individual assertion within and against the group. Each true jazz moment (as distinct from the uninspired commercial performance) springs from a contest in which each artist challenges all the rest; each solo flight, or improvisation, represents (like the successive canvases of a painter) a definition of his identity: as individual, as member of the collectivity and as a link in the chain of tradition." For Holiday, it would have gone without saying that one also played with and against the conventions and techniques of the music itself. Whether improvising on a traditional twelve-bar blues song, a pop ballad, or a show tune, Holiday the jamming musician would comment on solos by preceding players and have dialogues with those accompanying her solo statements. The jam session was a communal atelier, a highly ritualized place of artistic colloquy involving demonstrations, declamations, imitations, leapfrogging exchanges, love talk, parody, tomfoolery, boasting, and just plain "counting the dozens" (i.e., playing a competitive game of expression that tests who is most eloquently expressive under the guns of sometimes murderously unflattering commentary). Whatever the pressures, the jam session player was expected to stylize the given tune's timbres and tempos, and then to improvise on its chordal changes until he or she had made it into a newly energized song of his or her own. "Tell *your* story" was Lester Young's famous encouragement to fellow jazz players. The apocryphal anecdote about Young goes that he once told a highly skilled imitator of another player's musical styles, "Man, you can't join the throng 'til you play your *own* goddamn song."

To play with and against is the jazz mode. Given a song with flat lyrics or a dull melody, Holiday would parody it, as Whitney Balliett has observed, pronouncing each word with a biting "mixture of clarity and caricature, bringing into action that rule of ridicule that the victim be reproduced perfectly before being destroyed.... Her 'moons' and 'Junes' rang like bells, and one didn't hear their cracks until the sound began to die away." She would "turn a song completely around." Or, when a song had a more believable tune and lyrics, she would caress it, scratching and pressing it with her fingertips "as one does the head and spine of a favorite cat." If melody and/or the lyrics were weak, she would use her voice-as-horn not just to counterstate but to transcend the material. Such a brilliant jazz artist was easily bored, said drummer Chico Hamilton, who played with Lady many times. To make a song more musically interesting, she would "turn it around." She and Lester Young took "Me, Myself and I" (an impossibly contrived bit of juvenilia) and made it both believable and swinging. Playing with and against the song and each other, they swing "Me, Myself and I" and swing it hard. They swing it to life.

When Holiday hit New York in about 1930, she was fifteen but older than her years. It was not just because of hard times but because she had gone through "ordeals" in music that had put her well on the way toward finding her own sound and achieving her identity as an artist.

In New York, she took up where she had left off in Baltimore, looking for the night people and places where she could sing. The bigger city's night scene was flourishing. The reed player Kenneth Hollon, who later made records backing Holiday (including "Strange Fruit" and "Yesterdays"), was living on Pacific Street in the heart of the Bedford-Stuyvesant section of Brooklyn. His recollection was that when Holiday first hit New York, she and her mother had a small place on Granada Street in Brooklyn:

> Her mother was working in service. And all Billie wanted to do was sing. I was just learning to play my clarinet, and I used to take my saxophone around to her house. And I used to try to play melodies while she sang along with me. An opportunity came where we got a job out at this cabaret. And I took Billie along with us and once we were going good I asked Billie if she wanted to join in. "Yeah," she said, she did. And at that time I remember the old-timers used to throw money out on the floor for singers. And the tunes she sang that night were "My Fate Is in Your Hands" by Fats Waller and "Oh, How Am I to Know?" and "Honeysuckle Rose." And that night she collected over a hundred dollars in tips.

As Hollon told it, she performed on that first night out with a piano, drum, trumpet, and Hollon's sax. The place was in Brooklyn and was called the Grey Dawn. It attracted a hardened crowd of sportsmen and gamblers, a fast-living group that could drop large bills on the floor and not miss them as they drank their bootleg gin and dug the music. Just as the gray dawn actually arrived outside the club, the place was raided. Everybody on the bandstand was locked up, he said, except Holiday. Somehow in the confusion of the bust, she managed to trip away. After that night, Hollon and Holiday gigged in after-hours places all over Brooklyn and Queens for about two years, from 1930 to 1932.

Most witnesses of these early Holiday years, including Holiday herself, have placed her not in Brooklyn or Queens but in upper Manhattan, in Harlem. (It could be, of course, that the young hopeful paid a nickel each way and rode the train between the boroughs, gigging on both sides of the city's rivers, perhaps even on the same night.) According to several observers, Holiday arrived in New York from Baltimore and first took a room with her mother at Clara Winston's place at 135 West 142nd Street in Harlem. Within the same building, Winston had two adjoining apartments, one for herself and roomers and another that was run much like Ethel Moore's place in Baltimore—as an after-hours pad where people could buy food and drink, smoke reefer, dance, and buy sex.

"A big school girl" is what the comedian Pigmeat Markham saw when he first met Holiday in those early days. To Buck Clayton, she looked like one of those "big healthy farm girls" he had known back in Kansas. "But slicker," he said. "By the time I met her she was country-looking but city slick." She had grown up in the fast lane in Baltimore, not exactly a sleepy rural town. To her mother's dismay, Holiday quickly fit in at Clara Winston's place. Sadie was the housekeeper at Clara's, and Billie was all too eager to help out, too. The fifteen-

Connie's Inn, one of Harlem's premier nightclubs, c. 1937.

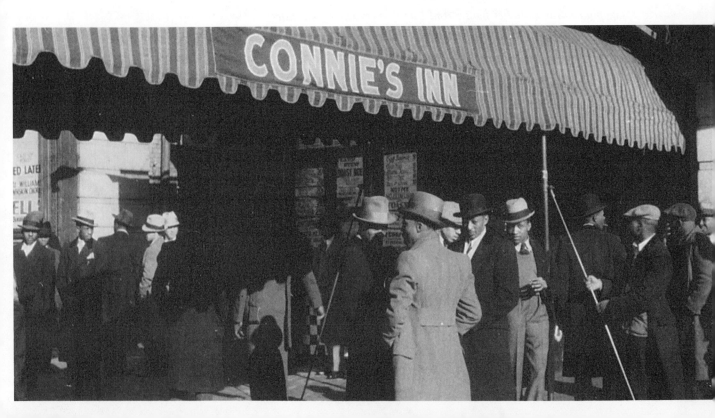

year-old liked to mingle with the night customers, serving food and drinks, and when Mama was not around, she would pour herself a glass of gin or roll a stick of marijuana. She also claimed that she would turn a few tricks to earn some extra dollars. Years later, Clara Winston said that she was not sure about that part of the story. All that she would say was "Better to sell it than to give it away."

Holiday quickly looked up her father and met him on jobs around town. So often was she among the women waiting for Fletcher Henderson's musicians to be through for the night that those musicians who did not know her already felt sure that she was just one of Clarence's many girlfriends.

"That's some daughter you've got," John Hammond told Clarence after hearing her at Monette's in 1933.

"You mean Billie?" Clarence asked, pulling Hammond off to one side. "Yeah, she is. But look here, now. Please don't be mentioning that she's my daughter to anybody, see? She's just something I stole when I was seventeen years old." Never having heard such talk, and misunderstanding the motives of playboy Clarence, who did not want any of his girlfriends to know he was old enough have such a grown-looking daughter, Hammond recoiled in horror. He remembered saying nothing more to Clarence about Billie, whom he thought the guitarist had crassly rejected.

Pigmeat Markham, 1950s.

The truth is that despite everything, Clarence was proud of his Billie. He took her around to the Rhythm Club and the Band Box, places where musicians and other show people could relax, free from the public eye. Eventually she was even old enough to meet him at Big John's Café on Seventh Avenue in Jungle Alley. "During the late twenties," writes George Hoefer, Big John's "was a daily hangout for the members of the Fletcher Henderson, Duke Ellington, and Fess Williams bands." Henderson's brother Horace, also a piano player and bandleader, composed "Big John's Special"— recorded by Count Basie's and other bands — in honor of the proprietor, who liked musicians and kept a pot of his "special" simmering for any musician in need of a free meal.

Trombonist J. C. Higginbotham, who played in the Henderson band during this period, remembered Big John's as "the first place I met Billie. We used to go there after hours, bring our own instruments, and just play. Clarence was playing banjo. She came alone. I introduced myself to her. She told me she was his daughter. Billie made a very good first impression, and it stayed like that. She didn't strike me as a fresh kid. She'd sit around and sing at Big John's just like we'd sit around and play." Other musicians have said that the teenage Billie Holiday was quiet and shy, but that if she got the chance to sing, she would

take it. She loved to be in relaxed settings and informal jam sessions where she could exchange choruses with a piano player or one or two of the horns. Benny Carter knew Clarence Holiday from the Henderson band, in which they had joined forces for a brief period. In 1930 or 1931, he saw Clarence's daughter for the first time at The Bright Spot on Seventh and 139th, "about a block from my house." Carter remembered, "It was a jam session place, and I stopped in frequently to hear Billie sing. There was no doubt that the informality of the setting, the freewheeling improvised blowing by the many fine musicians sitting in made a definite impression on Billie's singing style. I felt then that she had a touch of greatness in her."

"In those days," Holiday later said, "everything that happened, happened at a jam session somewhere.... It was at one of these sessions I first met Lester Young." He had come to town in 1934 to join the Henderson band before he joined Count Basie's group as a regular. "From then on," Holiday said, "Lester knew how I used to love to have him come around and blow pretty solos behind me. So whenever he could, he'd come by the joints where I was singing, to hear me or sit in." By 1934, Young and Holiday were tight friends but never lovers, as some accounts have it. "They were the brother and sister type," Carmen McRae explained. They would see each other and just get excited. They would hug and then lean close together talking the private jive talk for which Young was famous. Sadie Fagan, who adored Young and whom Young adored, rented him a room in the apartment with Billie and her. She was just one of the people who thought Billie and Young sounded somewhat alike. Sadie even told one interviewer that sometimes Billie would be humming a tune in the next room and at first she'd think it was Young practicing his horn. Both were coolly lyrical and playfully laid-back about the beat; both were vigorously inventive. Certainly Young would not have disagreed with the spirit of this statement by Holiday: "I can't stand to sing the same song the same way for two nights in succession, let alone two years or ten years. If you can, then it ain't music, it's close-order drill or exercise or yodeling or something, not music."

Whether or not she had made her New York debut in Harlem, by 1934 Billie had played nearly every joint there. Elmer Snowden said that he first heard her in an after-hours hangout called Goldgraben's. John Hammond caught her act at Monette's and later at Dickie Wells' Clam House, where the notorious Detroit Red worked with Holiday going table to table as singing waitresses and where (contrary to Holiday's own account) the young Baltimorean became skillful at doing what Red and the other Clam House singers were

Lester Young, 1937. Even before they joined forces in the Basie band and on the Teddy Wilson recording dates, Young and Holiday were close friends. Both withdrawn and painfully shy in their personal lives, they were artists of the highest caliber who loved the informal jam session settings where they could express themselves as they performed with and against their musical peers. (facing page)

George "Pops" Foster, 1937.

famous for: hiking up her dress to pick up tips between her legs as she sang to the customers one by one. Lawrence Lucie recalls hearing Holiday at the Ubangi Club, where she did a knockout job on "Them There Eyes." "All these years later," he said in 1991, "I can still hear that girl sing that song. She was original; she was outstanding. Always did have a different sound." Harry "Sweets" Edison said he first heard her at the Yeah Man Club. For many people, however, the first chance to hear her came when she played the Hot Cha and then Pod's and Jerry's.

At Pod's and Jerry's, Holiday played with Bobby Henderson and sometimes other piano players. For a while, she was part of a floor-show team organized by the Louisiana-born bass player George "Pops" Foster. Foster would open the show with his pattering jokes and jive. He would then introduce Charles "Honi" Coles, the precise and blindingly speedy rhythm tap man, who would perform solo or with Henderson's piano. Laurence D. Jackson came on next. "Baby" Laurence was thirteen in 1934 and not yet the jazz dancing phenomenon he would later become (largely through the assistance and example of Honi Coles). He was the group's "boy soprano" who performed a cappella versions of dramatic ballads and pop songs. "I would always have Billie close the show," Foster recalled. She had been a "stone hustler," he said, "but she found out she really could sing. She was our showstopper." Honi Coles remembered that she would do versions of things she later recorded. His first impressions of her probably were quite typical: "When I first heard Billie sing, it didn't move me at all. I was used to the Ethel Waters–type singing where you had clear singing and enunciation, and Billie kind of left me cold at first—until I listened a while and began to dig what bag she was in. I wound up liking her very much, *very* much." Sometimes the group was on salary, but the real money came in tips. Holiday was fifteen and earning about fifty dollars a night, sometimes much more.

Teddy Wilson never saw the Foster-Coles-Laurence-Holiday group in action. According to Irene Kitchings, Wilson's wife at the time, Benny Carter had told them about the incredible new singer at Pod's and Jerry's, and they went by to hear what Holiday could do. In 1972, Wilson remembered her performance at Pod's and Jerry's in this way:

> *She had an excellent pianist named Bobby Henderson. And she took turns singing with a girl named Beverly White and the three took turns and were the whole show.... "Them There Eyes" was one of her popular numbers then. She was singing it and everyone would request*

it. Beverly White and Billie were as different as day and night, and on the same show the two were terrific. Beverly was a great ballad singer, I think one of my favorites that I ever heard. And Billie had this beautiful rhythm singing, you know, faster tunes.... Billie sang ballads, but I preferred her for the more bright tempos, the rhythm songs— what in those days we used to call the jump tunes.

Smiling at Holiday all through the set was John Hammond, also in the club that night. Hammond, who had first heard Teddy Wilson on a radio broadcast from Chicago and then been instrumental in bringing him to the East, already had arranged solo piano sessions for him at Columbia Records. As well as being an excellent musician who was respected equally by gut-bucket players-by-ear and improvisers who came out of the academy, Wilson was urbane, quiet, and college trained. He struck Hammond, "the militant integrationist,"

Teddy Wilson, c. 1937. Wilson performed with Holiday in most of the recording sessions of the late thirties and early forties. Holiday often named Wilson as a model accompanist who could create interesting figures behind her without getting in her way.

Holiday, August 1939, in a relaxed jam session–style setting (for *Life* magazine's "Life Goes to the Party" feature). Left to right: J. C. Higginbotham, unknown, Rex Stewart, Holiday, Harry Lim, Cozy Cole, Eddie Condon (in back), Max Kaminsky, and Oran "Hot Lips".

as the one to spearhead his efforts to integrate the jazz world. At the end of the evening, Hammond rushed over to Wilson, and brought him to the front of the club to meet Holiday.

"Maybe we can get you two to make some records together," Hammond said. Holiday had never heard this quiet, "colleged" Teddy Wilson play the piano, and she must have had her doubts. But urged on by Hammond, they agreed to meet the next day at the Wilsons' apartment, where there was a piano, to see what might unfold.

"She was young. She was robust, carefree, just like a big kid," Irene Kitchings recalled. When Holiday arrived at their place, Wilson had not returned home yet. "We just became friendly right there. She called me 'Renie. And she told me right there, 'Renie, I've met a lot of wives, Duke's wife and this one's wife. But you're the first wife I've met that seems real…. I can dig you, 'cause you are a real person.'" Eventually the two became close friends and collaborators. Kitchings herself was an excellent piano player. In fact, Carmen McRae (in the hyperbolic mode) even said that she was a better pianist than Wilson. She became a songwriter as well. Her song "Some Other Spring" (which Holiday said was about the end of Kitchings's marriage to Wilson) was first presented by Holiday and is the one number she most often named as her favorite. Kitchings also wrote "Ghost of Yesterday" and "I'm Pulling Through," unusual, remarkable songs associated with Holiday.

On the day of the arranged meeting with Holiday, Wilson came home with a clutch of new song sheets under his arm. He told Holiday that he already had a contract with Brunswick to do some small-band dates. This guy Hammond had been some sort of classical music player, he told her, an amateur violist who dug chamber music stuff. He wanted something like a jazz chamber music sound, with Holiday's voice adding a burnished timbre to the ensemble. They would play authentic jazz, though, with the best cats in town being brought in to play with them. It could be Lester Young, Ben Webster, or Johnny Hodges —whoever was available. He told her that for the first recording session using her as the vocalist, Hammond had promised to bring in Benny Goodman. Holiday may not have been too keen on joining forces with Goodman again. The session in 1933 had sparked a short love affair that had ended abruptly. But she was game to look through song sheets—one of her favorite pastimes—and the idea of recording some more songs was quite exciting. And hey, this guy Teddy Wilson was a helluva good rocking and pretty-playing cat.

For that first Holiday-Wilson recording date in 1935, Hammond wanted to fight off any accusations of sloppiness from top management, so he had Wilson assemble the musicians a day ahead of time to run through the material and fix the introductory and closing figures for each piece. After that first time, however, the musicians did not rehearse before showing up for the recording sessions.

In fact, Buck Clayton, Jo Jones, and others who eventually played on the Wilson-Holiday recording dates loved to point out that they did not rehearse for them. They would arrive at the studio, and Wilson would announce a song, show the short introduction and ending he had arranged, and tell the order of solos. The band might do a run-through while Holiday was off by herself, looking at the song's lyrics. Then they would "hit," as musicians say. For the first few sessions, there were no second takes because Brunswick was on shaky financial ground and provided engineers for just one take. Jazz expert Albert Murray has commented on the lack of rehearsals and second takes at these sessions:

> *Many people marvel at the fact that not a lot of rehearsal was involved*
> *in the production of a number of really fine Billie Holiday records. It's*
> *marvellous mainly because the records sound so good, but the process is*

not marvellous at all. The musicians simply lived the music at all times. She was working with people whose styles and whose approaches and whose feelings and whose values she knew.... When you hear Lester go this way, you have something to go with it. It's just like talking to a bunch of friends. You know what's going to happen. Or you can do that with a bunch of enemies. You know what they're going to say, and you're primed and cocked for them.... That's why so many jam sessions record so well.

The first great Billie Holiday period was her jam session/after-hours period, when she did not attend lessons or rehearsals per se; rather, *she lived in terms of the music at all times.* A regular at Big John's and at informal jam sessions all over town, she, like the other musicians involved, was always prepared for the relaxed give-and-take of the Holiday-Wilson sessions. Had she been expected to sing within a tightly arranged framework with nonjazz musicians who did not know how to improvise, she might have faltered. But these sessions were set up in precisely the same way as the ones she had been singing in for about five years. To achieve the jam session–like sense of freedom and excitement that went with the collaborative music making of professional jazz players, Wilson called no rehearsals with the other musicians: "They'd just come to the record dates and because of the extemporaneous nature of the records, there was no need for rehearsals. These were all expert improvisers."

"For me not present at Billie's 1930's recording sessions," writes Gunther Schuller, "it remains mysterious as to how she learned these hundreds of songs— and so impeccably. The question arises not out of mere idle curiosity; it is a valid issue: first, because of the technical perfection of her performances.... Second, it is not possible to so thoroughly recompose and improvise upon that many songs without knowing them completely." Here again Murray's answer serves: she was a jazz musician whose art form required quick improvisation, and she was practicing the art of improvisation all the time. In this sense, she was related to both Louis Armstrong and John Coltrane, who reportedly kept their horns at their bedside while they slept so that they could pick them up first thing in the morning or even try out new ideas that awakened them in the middle of the night.

The other key biographical fact about Holiday that has heretofore gone unreported is that Wilson and Holiday, and later Irene Kitchings and Holiday, would get together the day before a recording session and go over possible songs. What else would a smart college boy do? Wilson remembered:

I would get together with Billie first, and we would take a stack of music, maybe thirty, forty songs, and go through them, and pick out the ones that would appeal to her—the lyric, the melody. And after we picked them we'd concentrate on the ones we were going to record. And we rehearsed them until she had a very good idea of them in her mind, in her ear…. Her ear was phenomenal, but she had to get a song into her ear so she could do her own style on it. She would invent different little phrases that would be different melody notes from the ones that were written. All great singers do that, do variations on the melody. Of course they have to know the melody inside out in order to do that. One afternoon would be sufficient to go through thirty, forty songs, and she would usually do three on a record date, though sometimes she would do four. And we would take an hour before the session on the ones we were going to record. We did this at my apartment because I had a piano…. We'd do it in the afternoons, after two, because we were working at night and slept during the day.

The Commodore recording session for "Strange Fruit," April 20, 1939. Left to right: John Williams, Holiday, Milt Gabler, Sonny White, and Kenneth Hollon.

So the mystery is not so mysterious after all. Wilson did collaborate with Holiday in choosing the songs and in helping her learn (so she could alter) the melodies.

It is important to know that Holiday was not just singing whatever songs she was given, as most accounts report. While it is clear that she sometimes was stuck at the last minute with a song that Columbia insisted she do to honor an obligation to a publisher or song plugger, she usually had some choice in these matters. According to Wilson, the two of them rejected 90 percent of the material they reviewed. What criteria would she use to reject songs? "When the melody was obviously too trite…trite lyrics, clichéd rhymes, and all that," Wilson said. "Most of the songs we did weren't hits, but they were pretty good songs. We tried to have both good lyrics and good melody."

Kitchings said that Holiday used to come up to their apartment to rehearse "all the time." Sometimes a bassist and drummer would join Holiday and Wilson. "I put padding under the drummer's feet, and they rehearsed," Kitchings remembered. Once Holiday was well known, if the police came to ask the band to quiet down, Kitchings would meet the officer at the door. "I said to this policeman, 'This is Billie Holiday. You know who she is, right?' 'Oh yeah, yeah.' 'Well, she's rehearsing for her next record date,' I said. 'I'm a widow woman.' And Lady would back me up, and she said, 'We're trying to help her out so I'm paying her for giving me a place to rehearse.'" The Wilsons had a very spacious apartment, the opposite of a desperate case. "And the policeman looked around and must've thought, 'What the hell, she doesn't need any help.' But nevertheless, he just said, 'Keep it down, keep it soft.' And left."

The first Holiday-Wilson recording date — July 2, 1935 — went incredibly well. To kick off the series, Hammond assembled "the best band that ever was." In addition to Holiday, Wilson, and the promised Benny Goodman, the band consisted of Roy Eldridge (trumpet), Ben Webster (tenor sax), Cozy Cole (drums), John Kirby (bass), and John Truehart (guitar). Hammond had convinced representatives of Columbia's Brunswick label that it needed black "covers" of pop songs already done by white singers to meet the demand of the burgeoning jukebox market in black neighborhoods. Since the publishing companies already had their "straight" versions of songs by singers such as Ginger Rogers and Bing Crosby, they did not care much what Hammond and his jazz groups did. The dates were cheap — five or six musicians at fifty dollars each, no royalties (almost no one got royalties in those days; musicians liked to record to advertise their club or theater appearances) — so how could the company lose? Aside from Hammond, no one from Brunswick showed up to "supervise," so the musicians could just follow Wilson's and Holiday's lead in making the music precisely the way they wished. When it came to accompanying Holiday, Wilson said, "I played fill-in type things. I let her carry the melody. I never led her. I never would play the melody along with them. And when she'd pause, I'd play some figure, some fill-in thing. Which left her all the freedom in the world to sing any phrase any way she wanted."

Holiday at the Off-Beat Club, Chicago, 1939, with Jimmy McPartland's band.

(facing page)

An itinerary written by Holiday, whose spelling was often uncertain. It shows the tight schedule of the fall of 1958, as she moved from Milwaukee to Monterey. She was careful to note when and where she was to perform and the name of the "boss" involved. Recordings prove that she was in excellent form for Monterey, just nine months before her death. Commenting on her style of this period, Dan Morgenstern said, "Some say that what Billie does now is no longer singing. Whatever it is, it sure as hell communicates."

To be sure she got the words right, she held the music sheets while she recorded "I Wished on the Moon," "What a Little Moonlight Can Do," and "Miss Brown to You." Benny Goodman had an appointment downtown and was not with the band when it did "A Sunbonnet Blue (and a Yellow Straw Hat)." Perhaps, as Michael Brooks has surmised, Goodman had taken one look at the song's lead sheet (Wilson and Holiday must have figured they could override its dullness) and decided to cut out. Despite this highly unconvincing ditty, the session sparkled—with three big winners the first time out. Holiday's voice was effervescent, full of the joy of invention and spirited conversation in the up-tempo jazz idiom. Here was "jump tune" Billie Holiday, jam session readied for this date with the giants, proving herself to be their equal. To paraphrase Rudolf Nureyev on what great dancers can do—she had made the hard passages sound easy and the easy passages sound interesting.

Between 1935 and 1942 ("when," as Leonard Feather said, "Billie's relationship with Columbia and its affiliate labels was cut short by a waning interest on the part of her employers and by the practical reality of the recording ban"), Holiday cut hundreds of titles for Columbia. Most of them featured Wilson, though eventually, much to her delight, she recorded under the name "Billie Holiday and Her Orchestra" and sometimes used pianists other than Wilson. In each case, the dates would be set up with the idea of assembling an all-star band that, as in jam sessions, played together only on special occasions. Wilson, Hammond, and eventually Holiday worked together to decide who, among the musicians in town at the time, they wanted to use for the upcoming session. Usually they drew from the Basie, Ellington, Goodman, or Teddy Hill bands. She came to prefer the Basie guys, particularly Lester Young and Buck Clayton.

What she liked most about them was that like Wilson, they would not compete with her so much as they would "fill up the windows," as Clayton put it in a 1990 interview. "I didn't want to obstruct anything that she did," he said. He continued:

And if she had a special, pretty phrase, I wouldn't play in there until she came to the end of the phrase. Then I would fool around a little bit—what we'd call "fill up the windows." I wouldn't do that unless I was sure her phrase was over. I think that's why she liked for me to play with her 'cause I didn't get in her way.... I'd watch her lips. And when her lips would close, I'd make a little...musical figure there. When her lips would open up again, I'd shut up.

This "first Holiday" period's greatness sprang from her credentials not just as a star soloist but as a collaborator in a jazz band setting. Her most successful partners in this collaboration were able, as Wilson and Clayton said, to complement her work by finishing her musical phrases with patterns of their own, by making her melodic lines a continuous thread of invented sound. Clayton's playing on "Me, Myself and I" is a fine example of this magnificent calling and recalling, this "filling up the windows" with sound.

At times the complementary additions of her musical cohorts consisted of their improvised playing behind her melodic line. Lester Young was great at this. On certain pieces, he seems to be humming behind her, showing off her solo statements by dropping behind her his own beautifully billowing curtain of sound. Check out the fabulously simpatico work on "I'll Never Be the Same." Yet another strategy of accompaniment brought to perfection in these Wilson-Holiday sides was that of creative contrast. This is where Wilson was a master. As listeners, we go with Holiday on an exhilarating ride through melody that defines Whitney Balliett's excellent description of great jazz music: "the sound of surprise." Behind Holiday's voice, and then in the solo light, is Wilson's piano: his work satisfies not so much by the derring-do of his new inventiveness—that is Holiday's forte—as by his rhythmic sureness, the wittiness of his intimations of melody, and the tasteful sparkle of his chordal voicings.

Jazz is the most democratic of the arts, and these group creations define democracy in action. Six or eight geniuses were in the recording studio. Each one was encouraged to express his or her individual thoughts and feelings. At the same time each worked as part of a coherent and mutually supportive ensemble. It was *e pluribus unum* with a swinging beat.

The first Holiday period falls in the early years of her recording at Columbia, from 1935 to 1939. During that time, she made the indispensable sides that many Holiday lovers call her perfect records. Even then, no doubt because of her color, she was mislabeled a blues singer. In fact, she recorded only two blues songs during these years: "Billie's Blues" (1936) and "Long Gone Blues" (1939). The other songs she did were Tin Pan Alley songs and tunes from the movies or Broadway. Every Holiday fan who is familiar with this period has his or her own list of favorite titles. My list includes "It's Like Reaching for the Moon," "These Foolish Things," "I Cried for You," "Who Loves You," "I Can't Give You Anything But Love," "I Must Have That Man," "I'll Get By," "Foolin' Myself," "Me, Myself and I," "A Sailboat in the Moonlight," "Trav'lin' All Alone," "I'll Never Be the Same," "He's Funny That Way," "The Moon Looks Down

and Laughs," "Long Gone Blues," "Some Other Spring," "Them There Eyes," and "The Man I Love." These were the songs that helped a generation endure the trials of the Depression—not just with otherworldly fantasies, though she offered a few of those, too, but with danceable music that was alive with the quicksilver sound of a richly inventive artist exuberantly at work.

"She liked difficult songs, songs with something to them," Irene Kitchings said. These songs presented her with enough of a challenge for her to honor them, to accentuate their best features, but they also were interesting enough for her to transform. The odd thing about her being called a blues singer is that while she was certainly not a blues diva in the sense that Ida Cox was (almost all of Cox's records are framed in the twelve-bar blues format), she did transform her material, wherever it came from, with precisely the same readiness and zest for new invention that is associated with riffing on the blues. Like Coleman Hawkins confronting "Body and Soul," which in his famous 1939 recording he changed into a song by Hawkins as much as by J. Green, et al., the first Holiday recomposed these songs and made them part of the Billie Holiday songbook. Who else but Billie Holiday could do justice to "What a Little Moonlight Can Do"?

The year 1935 was a keystone for the first Holiday period. That was the year of her premiere at Harlem's Apollo Theater. A stagehand at the Apollo, Bob Hall, always claimed that he (and not Ralph Cooper, who also weighs in with his assertion of "discovering" Billie Holiday) was the one who heard her at the Alhambra Grill when "she really tore it up." As he told it, his recommendation secured Holiday a week's gig at the Apollo. It paid about thirty-five dollars. Pigmeat Markham, the veteran comedian, was yet another one who modestly admitted having "discovered" Holiday for the Apollo stage. He told the following apocryphal tale:

She was standing in the wings before she went on. The music come up. She froze, she just stood there. And I give her a shove, a hard shove, and I didn't intend to shove her as hard as I did, and I guess she would've fell, but she grabbed on to the mike and finally got herself together. And she started singing. She was singing a song called "If the Moon Turns Green."... And she sung "Them There Eyes"—that was her song in them days.... She tore that house down.... She stood in that green spot and she sang and sang and sang and sang. She was terrific. They wouldn't let her off the stage. I stood in the wings all the way through. She was stage-frighted 'cause she was used to playing

A still from Holiday's 1935 movie with Duke Ellington, *Symphony in Black*. Pushed to the ground by her two-timing lover, Holiday sings the "Big City Blues (The Saddest Tale)" in a voice that shows her kinship to Bessie Smith. (overleaf)

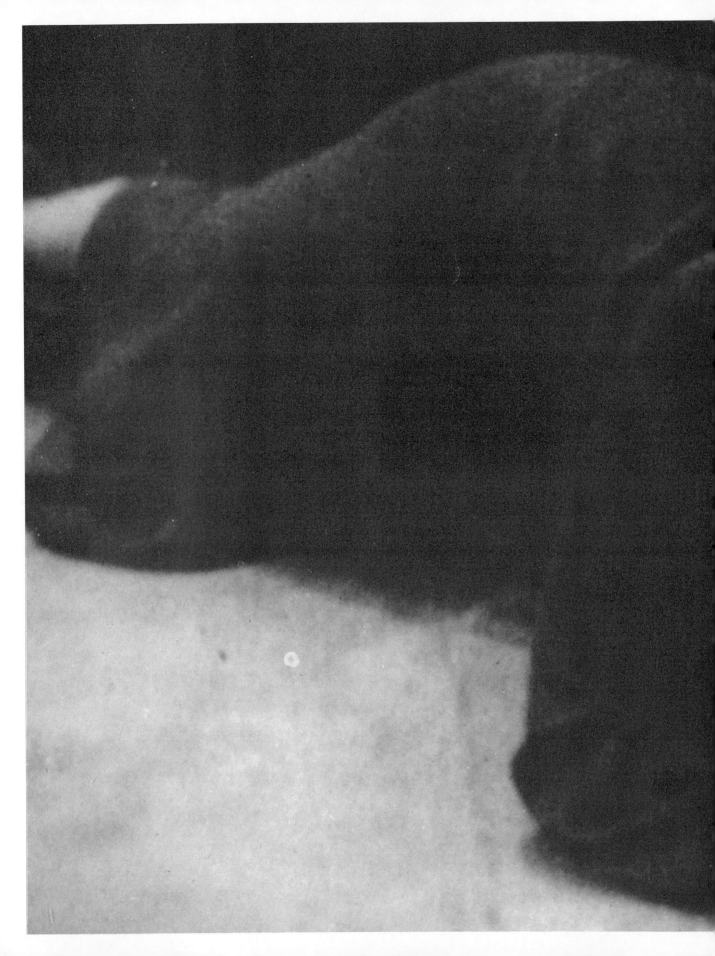

the small joints, you know. And when you're used to singing for twenty-five people and then you have a thousand, two thousand people, you freeze up. But she did it to death, she was terrific.

Earlier that year, Holiday had had the thrill of being approached to appear in a movie with Duke Ellington and his orchestra. *Symphony in Black* was a short film made to run with newsreels and other miscellaneous material before the feature film came on. (Perhaps the idea was to replace the bands that sometimes played between movie showings with films of bands.) In any case, *Symphony in Black* is a little-celebrated Ellington treasure, one of his glorious extended works in which twenty-year-old Billie Holiday appears as an incarnation of the blues in a section of the piece called "Blues."

In this movie, Holiday is unmistakably the star student of Bessie Smith. In the compressed, declamatory style she had practiced back in Baltimore when she would sing along with Smith's records, she delivers her lines to a tee. The elegance of Ellington's arrangement provides just the right showcase for Holiday's delicate but nonetheless powerful contralto. And it is wonderful to see young Holiday in

Holiday and Duke Ellington, c. 1945.

He once referred to her singing as

"the essence of cool."

action. Playing the part of an unglamorous street woman done wrong, she is not dressed or made up to flatter her looks. But the diamond-in-the-rough beauty, of both her voice and her body, is deep and irresistible.

In 1937, John Hammond invited Count Basie to come with him to hear the new singer at Clark Monroe's on 134th Street near Seventh Avenue, a downstairs place formerly known as Barron's. "That's when I heard Billie Holiday for the first time," Basie said. He continued:

> *And she was something. I was really turned on by her. She knocked me out. I thought she was so pretty. A very, very attractive lady. And when she sang, it was an altogether different style. I hadn't heard anything like it, and I was all for it, and I told John I sure would like to have her come and work with the band if it could be arranged. And naturally John agreed, because he already had the same idea before he took me to hear her. So he arranged it. I've forgotten what the terms were, but he and Willard Alexander worked it out, and she came with us. And she did so well that everybody immediately fell in love with her.*

This offer turned her on, too. She already knew several fellows in the band, having seen them on the club and jam session circuit. In January of that year, she had made the first of many Holiday-Wilson records with Basie band members Lester Young, Buck Clayton, and Walter Page. Guitarist Freddie Green, who joined Basie's band at about the same time she did, also was present on that recording session of January 1937. She and Young had been friends since he had come to New York back in 1934, and he had been the one to introduce her to Clayton, Jo Jones, and several others in the band. "When she joined Count Basie's band, it was one of the joys of our lives," Clayton said. "To have the great Billie Holiday singing with our band was something we never thought possible—a pleasure we never thought we would have. It was through John Hammond, and her acquaintanceship with me and Lester, that Billie joined Basie."

As a rhythm singer, she was just right for Basie's rhythm machine, wherein Basie (as Ralph Ellison has observed) would use the whole band as if it were a drum. Like Holiday, Basie specialized not just in the keeping of flawless tempos but in the magic of musical understatedness. Both as a soloist and an arranger, Basie kept things to a minimum, never using two notes where one would do.

And his arrangements "opened the door" for his soloists in just the right way to show off their talents to the greatest advantage. Like Holiday, too, many of Basie's musicians played by ear, memorizing "head arrangements" worked out by the group under Basie's guidance. Holiday, who never learned to read music but who "had ears," felt right at home in their midst.

According to Harry "Sweets" Edison, the number "Swing, Brother, Swing" was an arrangement by that keystone Basie collaborator Eddie Durham, who tailor-made it for Holiday. On that number, recorded live at the Savoy, we hear the first Holiday in her role as the "Lady Who Swung the Band." Her vocal incantations excite the ensemble into supercharged rhythmical action that seems, particularly because of the use of the word *brother,* a highly secular version of what Winthrop Sargeant called the "rhythmo-dramatic" activity of a shout-stirred religious assembly. You can almost see and hear the dancers stomping and shuffling on the floor as she beats out the words:

> *Deep rhythm captivates me;*
> *Hot rhythm stimulates me.*
> *Can't help but swing it, boys;*
> *Swing it, Brother, Swing.*

Left to right: Lester Young and

Jo Jones.

Remembering those days with Holiday and Basie, Edison said, "She was a jazz singer. She had instant tonality. She had a fantastic ear. She had a fantastic conception of when to sing and how to place the words to make them swing.... She could swing *anything*.... If she couldn't swing, she couldn't have been in Basie's band, because he had the swingingest band in the land."

Holiday also did slow dance numbers with Basie. When she first joined the band, she had no music of her own scored for a big band; she had worked almost exclusively with small groups. She asked Clayton to put together an arrangement of "They Can't Take That Away from Me." On the air-check version of it, quite different from the one recorded in the studio, Clayton's orchestration (not unlike his own solo playing in other settings) "fills up the windows" and leaves plenty of room for Holiday to take the song where she wants to go. Again you can hear the tremendous exuberance in her voice, and again it seems to give this already high-spirited band an additional lift. The first Holiday was not just a small-combo swinger; she was becoming a skillful musician in the context of a big band—especially this band, where the 4/4 rhythms were as steady and strong as a highballing train and night after night she could trade riffs with Young, Clayton, Edison, and the man who could make a single note swing, Basie himself.

Left to right: Buck Clayton and
Herschel Evans.

THE MANY FACES OF BILLIE HOLIDAY • *Lady Day*

Precisely what it was that ended the collaboration between Holiday and Basie is unclear. Jo Jones insisted that she left the band because of pressure from John Hammond, who he said advised Basie to put her out because she would not sing blues songs in the greatest blues band in the world. According to Jones, Holiday was not particular about singing the blues, and she did not want to step on the toes of Jimmy Rushing, the band's blues specialist, who had been with Basie since before there was a Basie band. Jones said that Holiday sang rhythm numbers and ballads but left the blues to Rushing, whose blues had made him the band's number one attraction at the time.

Being the only woman on a bus traveling from one-nighter to one-nighter was a blast at first. Holiday had a boyfriend in the band, Freddie Green, one of her few nice-guy lovers. (Maybe she fell for him because she knew he was only temporarily available. He had made it clear that he liked to play around but that he was devoted to his wife and children back home. Then, too, he might have been of special interest because, like her father, he was an anchor-steady rhythm guitarist.) She grew closer and closer to her "brothers" in the band, Lester Young and Buck Clayton. After everyone else was asleep, she and Clayton would talk late into the night. If a group was awake, she would join them in a reefer or two and a crap game at the back of the bus.

"She was one of the boys," Clayton said, using a phrase they often applied to her. "We didn't have to watch our language because she could outcurse some of the guys."

"We *lived* on the bus," Edison said. If it was time to change clothes or call for an emergency stop of necessity, no one felt self-conscious about Holiday. She was family.

Holiday said that going from town to town, particularly in the South, where accommodations were uncertain at best, began to spoil the traveling party. But it was in the North that the rub came. At Detroit's Fox Theater, which had a strict whites-only admission policy, the band fell in and got ready to go on. But the theater's manager held things up until Holiday was properly made up. He felt that she appeared too light skinned to be singing with an obviously all-black band; some customers might have been offended. So she darkened her face. Some commentators have said that too much has been made of this "blacking up" after the fact and that at the time performers did such things without thinking much about them. But it was 1937, a period when black artists were becoming more and more aware of the social impact of the roles they were expected to play. It is easy to believe that "blacking up" in

New York's Strand Theater, 1948. Holiday was the featured singer with William "Count" Basie's band in 1937 and 1938. During their brief but significant association, prior contractual agreements kept them from making any records together, and only three airchecks survive to mark their efforts as a team. These recorded radio broadcasts show that theirs was a perfect marriage of musicians who could swing hard and who never used three notes when one or two could tell the story. After their split, Holiday and Basie remained friends and often performed together. She called him "Bill"; he called her "William." (facing page)

Detroit was part of what made Holiday think about heading back home. "It's like they say," she later quipped, "there's no damn business like show business. You had to smile to keep from throwing up."

For years Holiday complained that she'd been fired from the Basie band and that John Hammond had been behind it. Willard Alexander, an executive of the Music Association in America, gave a pointed version of what happened in the September 1938 issue of *Down Beat:* "It was John Hammond who got Billie the job with Count Basie, and he was responsible for Basie keeping her. In fact, if it hadn't been for John Hammond, Billie would have been through six months earlier." Why was she sacked? "The reason," Alexander said, "was strictly one of deportment, which was unsatisfactory, and a distinctly wrong attitude towards her work. Billie sang fine when she felt like it. We just couldn't count on her for consistent performance."

Whether or not Alexander's version is accurate, it is clear that the economics of the collaboration ceased to make sense. Because Basie and Holiday had contracts with different record companies, they could not make records together. Basie always said simply that she was becoming a star on her own and had begun to get offers that he could not begin to match. He said she had left with his blessing.

Holiday was with Basie for less than a year, but for her it was an unforgettable time. She remembered it as being longer: "For the two years I was with the band, we had a book of a hundred songs, and every one of us carried every last damn note of them in our heads."

In 1938, Holiday moved over to the Artie Shaw band, becoming one of the first (not the very first, as many accounts have it) blacks to appear as a regular featured vocalist with an otherwise all-white orchestra. Shaw, a clarinetist, had offered her the job eighteen months before and was overjoyed when she finally said yes. Despite the grave misgivings of his backers, who were not race crusaders but investors in the band as a money-making business, Shaw took Holiday to Boston's Roseland State Ballroom, where she was well received. Bookings beyond Boston proper, however, produced less enthusiasm for Holiday. The crowds treated her coldly. According to John Chilton, "Much of this indifference had nothing to do with racial prejudice; it was simply that Billie's style was too uncommercial for the casual listener to enjoy." Still, from the viewpoint of the musicians on the bandstand, things were never better. Although the rhythms sometimes became too plodding (it was during this period that Shaw hired the black drummer Zutty Singleton to "coach" the band), the group's enthusiasm

Holiday, c. 1940. With Billy Eckstine.

(top) **With friends.** (bottom)

and earthiness reminded Holiday of Basie's group. *Down Beat* reviewed her with Shaw in June 1938: "Her lilting vocals gibe beautifully with the Shaw style.... Most of all the personality and musicianship of this real jazz gal have won and unified the whole band, and these days more than one solo is being played straight at Billie."

Eventually, troubles on the road—exacerbated by the shocking sight of one gorgeous black woman traveling and performing with fourteen white men—again arose. Often Holiday could not get a room in the hotels where the rest of the band stayed, and she could not eat and drink with them in white restaurants and cafés. Sometimes her white colleagues would prevail in their insistence that Holiday be treated fairly, but the struggle became wearing. "It wasn't long," she said, "before the roughest days with the Basie band began to look like a breeze. I got to the point where I hardly ever ate, slept, or went to the bathroom without having a major NAACP-type production."

Some places simply would not book a white band with a black singer. And some song pluggers would not give Shaw's band their material to sing on radio shows because she changed their written tunes and was "too artistic." Shaw compromised and hired another singer, nineteen-year-old Helen Forrest. Inevitably, when Forrest was given material that had been arranged for Holiday, pressures mounted. To top it all off, contractual conflicts arose, and Holiday could not record with Shaw's band. The one song they were able to record, "Any Old Time," was quickly dropped from the Shaw catalog and redone by Forrest.

Racial slurs against Holiday could easily have led to physical violence. Band members recalled that one time the band had started its show in a southern hotel ballroom, with Holiday sitting onstage with Shaw and the others. A man shouted to Shaw, "When's blackie going to sing?" Holiday had the answer: "Get that motherfucker out here!" Shaw let the band play on but signaled to them to get ready to pack up and split in a hurry. They were in their cars and on the road before anything more happened. There can be no doubt that as much as Holiday may have wanted to let the big mouth feel the razor she carried in her stocking, she also knew that to do so could have brought a lynch mob together very quickly.

Holiday's own summarizing anecdote for why she left Shaw is quite significant. She said that after touring the country and encountering racial troubles off and on, the band was glad to be back in New York. They were to take up residency at the Lincoln Hotel in midtown. She walked into the hotel

Holiday with Frank Sinatra, who said that Holiday "was and still remains the greatest single musical influence on me." (top) Holiday with Basie and Henry Woode. (bottom)

and was told by the owner and manager, Theresa Kramer, that she could not enter by the front door but must go through the kitchen with the rest of the band. At that time, she told a reporter for the *Amsterdam News,* "Gee, we were really a big hit all over the South and never ran into the color question until we opened at the Lincoln Hotel here in New York City." She added: "I was billed next to Artie himself, but was never allowed to visit the bar or the dining room, as did the other members of the band. Not only was I made to enter and leave the hotel through the kitchen but had to remain alone in a little dark room all evening until I was called on to do my numbers. And these numbers became fewer and fewer as time went on." In a subsequent interview, she hit at Shaw himself, whom she felt had done nothing to help her in the Lincoln Hotel incident: "I simply got enough of Artie's snooty know-it-all mannerisms and the outrageous behavior of his managers and left the band." She went on to say that Shaw had never paid her as much as Basie had and that he owed her for the one song she had made with the band. "The real trouble was this," she said. "Shaw wanted me to sign a five year contract, and when I refused, it burned him." Shaw denied all of these charges, with the whole affair making national news.

Holiday never sang with Shaw after 1938, but she did sing with big bands again. She headlined with Lionel Hampton's group during 1940 and 1942, and she made special appearances with Basie. But by 1939, Holiday's first important period was over. She had become a star during those years and had cut records that were among the best she ever made. These were the jam session – chamber music records in which her experiences in the back rooms of Baltimore and Harlem, and onstage with Basie and Shaw, had crystallized her talent and made her into a singer who, still in her early twenties, was already one of the most powerful of the century. What the poet Michael Harper has said about John Coltrane also is true of Billie Holiday during this first period: Trane's music, wrote Harper, is "aggressive, for it grows out of a living experience; and his music is the total environment of the jam session, the jazz set as the expression of the interaction of forces, his present and past modalities. One's musicianship is not a technical maneuver but the equipment and the control to let the power flow, for the artist's responsibility is to create control, to call up symbols that give up the power, in modal forms, of that spirit which is man and universe."

RELEASE FROM

CAPP-JOHNSON *Publicity*

545 FIFTH AVENUE, NEW YORK CITY, 17

from: Greer Johnson

VA 6 - 0825-0826

EXCLUSIVE TO WALTER WINCHELL

For the second time in a month, St. Louis' popular Plantation Club has dealt tolerance and democracy a blow below the belt. This time it involves the great blues singer, Billie Holiday, whom Esquire magazine singled out this very month with a full-page color photograph and a caption lauding her as the outstanding singer of her field. Miss Holiday was scheduled to open at the Plantation last week, following a recent altercation over color in which a member of Benny Carter's band was severely injured by the blow of a pistol butt on the head. When the singer had finished the first show of her opening night, she prepared to leave the club with a white friend. This man had befriended her several years ago when she was in the city with Artie Shaw's band. The manager stopped them at the door, delivered several unpleasant remarks, and forcibly threw the white man out. When Miss Holiday returned for her second show, she was told to read the signs which forbid any "mixing". She was then told she needn't go on for the second show. At this writing, she is sitting in a St. Louis hotel, waiting for her manager (Joe Glaser) to arrive and straighten things out. The club has called her to return--but on the old terms of humiliation, scorn, and prejudice. A fine thing, that in the mother city of the river which gave jazz to the world, an outstanding figure of the jazz world should be ridiculed for the color of her skin!

One of the papers that carried the story of Billie Holiday's split with Artie Shaw mentioned that she was off to perform at a new place in the Village. That new place, at 2 Sheridan Square, was the Café Society, a club started by a Latvian American shoe salesman named Barney Josephson who had dreamed of starting a place modeled after European cabarets featuring good entertainment infused with subtly political charges. Josephson was a jazz fan whose burning ambition was to counter the segregated club scene, which typically involved all-black shows and white-only clientele, with a genuinely integrated place. He said, "I wanted a club where blacks and whites worked together behind the footlights and sat together out front. There wasn't, so far as I know, a place like it in New York or in the whole country." With money from friends who shared his views, including the omnipresent John Hammond, who was directly responsible for setting up the outstanding cast of jazz artists who would perform, Josephson opened the first Café Society. The club's name seemed to proclaim its snootiness, but the place itself had an air of artsy/intellectual/hip informality about it. When patrons arrived at the Café Society on opening night, December 18, 1938, a doorman greeted them in overformal style. He wore a tattered top hat and tails and a pair of spotless white gloves with the tips ripped off.

Holiday opened the Café Society's first show and remained at the club for more than a year. It was during that stay that the "second Holiday" (1939 to 1949) was born. Many Holiday fans believe that this was her greatest era. During this span, she often performed in the city or out of town in settings precisely like the ones she had known in her earlier years. When she sang with

Lionel Hampton's band, for example (in 1941 at the Palace Theater in Cleveland on the same bill with the teenager Dinah Washington, who was always in awe of Lady Day), she swung that already swinging band as it had never been swung before. She played the Apollo every year, sometimes sharing the stage, or at least the marquee, with Duke Ellington, Count Basie, Fletcher Henderson, and even her old hero and mentor-by-record, Louis Armstrong.

But a change had come. The beginning of this change may be marked by her starting to sing the song that propelled her into the ranks of the "crossover" stars: "Strange Fruit." Throughout her life, Billie Holiday would claim that the song began as a poem written especially for her and that she and her Café Society pianist, Sonny White, wrote the music. The truth is that Lewis Allen, a New York schoolteacher, wrote both the melody and the lyrics. His idea was to compose a work that dramatized his hatred of lynching and, once he had written it, to present the piece to public gatherings and politicized social sets. The words of "Strange Fruit" are as follows:

> *Southern trees bear a strange fruit:*
> *Blood on the leaves and blood at the root;*
> *Black bodies swinging in the southern breeze;*
> *Strange fruit hanging from the poplar trees.*
>
> *Pastoral scene of the gallant South:*
> *The bulging eyes and the twisted mouth;*
> *Scent of magnolia sweet and fresh;*
> *Then the sudden smell of burning flesh.*
>
> *Here is a fruit for the crows to pluck;*
> *For the rain to gather, for the wind to suck.*
> *For the sun to rot, for the tree to drop;*
> *Here is a strange and bitter crop.*

Allen showed Josephson the song sheet for the work, which had already been performed by singers at leftist gatherings for about a year. Josephson felt that the song might fit in well with the club's "political" theme and that Holiday was the one to sing it.

Another idea also appealed to him—that of having a black woman sing her series of show tunes and Tin Pan Alley numbers, along with a blues number or two,

Holiday at a record session, 1940.

(top, facing page)

Left to right: Holiday, Kermit Scott, Roy Eldridge, Sonny White, and John Williams. (middle, facing page)

Left to right: Sonny White, Roy Eldridge, John Williams, Harold "Doc" West, Kermit Scott, Jimmy Powell, Carl Frye, and Lawrence Lucie. (bottom, facing page)

Holiday at Greenwich Village's Café Society, 1939. Set up as an integrated club, it attracted leftists, jazz lovers, and New Yorkers in the know. Even Eleanor Roosevelt once visited the swinging little club. It was here that Holiday began to sing "Strange Fruit," her signature song of this period.

and then end with an overt protest song. Doubtless, too, he saw the dramatically effective incongruity of having this protest song about lynchings down South presented by this loveliest of women, now known for her silks and lace and her overall aristocratic bearing, someone who at first seemed light-years away from such concerns but who nonetheless served up the song with excruciating vividness.

Josephson said that when he showed the song to Billie Holiday, she was not too sure of its value for her. But she and her piano player went through it, as she always did with new songs. And as always, she learned the song's melody and then radically altered it, compressing it into her best range and concentrating its power. In this sense, Holiday the recomposer did write the song herself, just as she wrote other Holiday inventions such as "Summertime" and "I Cried for You." Whatever the name on the sheet music, "Strange Fruit" became an unmistakable part of Billie Holiday's artistic territory. It gave her a vehicle that worked because of the stark contrast between her elegance and the song's anger. Indeed this anger, which had seethed below the surface of many "love" songs of her first period, now became unsparingly direct and searing. Good art must be "hard," said Henry James, "as hard as nails, as hard as the heart of the artist." And while her timbre and timing, her whole way with a song, identified her as part of an African American tradition of singing (with, to be sure, its European and other influences as well), "Strange Fruit" was the only song she had ever sung that gave direct expression to her identity as an African American of political consciousness. Furthermore, that song, with its imagery of trees that "bear" and "fruit" that is "plucked" or "dropped," also gave expression to her role as a woman who discerned a sexual motive in the act of lynching. "I am a race woman," she often said. And you could feel the integrity and the uncompromising power of her words.

In interviews, she would spell out her personal connection with the song by telling people about her father, Clarence Holiday, who had died unexpectedly two years before she began to present the song. He had been touring Texas with Don Redman's band when he caught what seemed to be nothing more than a cold. As a result of having suffered permanent damage to his lungs from gas poisoning in World War I, however, he knew that he needed special care when even the smallest respiratory problem arose. But he also knew that the year was 1937 and the place was Texas. He decided that rather than risk refusal or second-class service based on his color, he would wait until the band reached Dallas's veterans hospital. The delay was too long, however, and not long after being admitted to the hospital, he died of pneumonia. Billie was crushed by the news

The Café Society, 1939.

of her father's death and always said that "Strange Fruit" reminded her that her father had been "lynched" by the South's racism. She also said that she had to keep on singing the song because "things like this are still happening."

The first time Holiday sang "Strange Fruit" at the Café Society, she "thought it was a mistake. There wasn't even a patter of applause when I finished. Then a lone person began to clap nervously. Then suddenly everyone was clapping." To emphasize the song's impact, Josephson got Holiday to close every set with it. His instructions were that no one ring the cash register during the song and that waiters stand still and wait until she finished. The club was dark except for a pin of light trained on Holiday's face. When the song ended, the lights went completely out for a moment. No matter what the applause, there were no encores. Musicians have said that sometimes after a performance of "Strange Fruit," Holiday would be in tears and stay in an emotional state for some time before she was able to pull herself together.

Many commentators, notably John Hammond, have felt that "Strange Fruit" marked the end of Holiday's greatness, that after that song, she turned

Holiday with pianist Jess Stacy and a friend, 1941.

from a swinging chamber music or big band style and embraced the pose of a torch singer. According to this view, the first Holiday sold out and became a mannered *artiste* warbling "meaningfully" for rich, if left-leaning, white folks. Others argue that the song was a failure because her great talents were exploited for political causes, that the nightclub's ritual of fertility and purification was subverted by artless ends when people who came out looking to have a good time and blow the blues away found themselves hammered at by a self-pitying woman wailing about black death in the South. Gunther Schuller, however, has defended "Strange Fruit" as more than just a song: "It is a powerfully moving document and monument to Billie's artistry—and guts. It is also a fine unpretentious composition in B-flat minor, a key Chopin and other composers knew how to use well for their more sombre pieces.... It is a mark of the depth and breadth of her artistry that, without any drastic modifications, her basic style embraced this sombre opus too."

While in a sense this song may have represented a continuation of her "basic style," it also marked a significant new departure. This was the second Holiday. She was not only the rhythm singer and reinventor of ballads such as "You Can't Take That Away from Me"; she had made herself into a vocal actress who could present "Strange Fruit" and other slow poem/songs with tremendous dramatic tension. One way of looking at this new departure is to examine the "Strange Fruit" recording session and the other sides she did for Commodore Records on that day in April 1939. How did she come to record them, when she was under contract to Columbia Records?

Café Society customers started asking Holiday if they could buy records of "Strange Fruit" or expect to hear it on the radio or on jukeboxes. Although Hammond had been willing to record the song, Columbia's top brass, fearing a negative reaction from the southern white market, vetoed the project. Early in the spring of 1939, Holiday stopped by the Commodore Music Shop, Manhattan's premier store for current as well as rare jazz records, and talked to the owner, Milt Gabler. She knew that Gabler had begun not just selling records but also producing them under his own label, Commodore Records. She also knew that his catalog showed taste and daring. By 1939, Commodore had pressed the outstanding Willie "The Lion" Smith solo sides and the excellent Kansas City Six records featuring Holiday's old friends Lester Young, Buck Clayton, Freddie Green, Jo Jones, Walter Page, and Eddie Durham. Commodore also had reissued excellent piano solos by Teddy Wilson and a so-so session by Fletcher Henderson featuring the guitar of Clarence Holiday.

Holiday was known for her dogs, which she would sometimes call her "children." She often made dramatic nightclub exits and entrances with them in arms or on leashes. Doubtless the dogs were part of the costume of a woman who was intensely private and knew how to keep people at a distance.

Billie with Jimmy Monroe, her first husband, c. 1940.

"Milt, what do you think?" Holiday asked Gabler. "Columbia won't let me record 'Strange Fruit.'"

He immediately thought Commodore could do the job. And he thought that since his shop sold Columbia records and all of his Commodore records were pressed at Columbia's facilities, a deal could be arranged.

"Why don't you go up to Columbia," he told Holiday. "You tell them it's a little record dealer, has its own label, and see if they'll let you make it for me. Let them give you permission to do one session, which would be four tunes." Holiday walked the block over to Columbia and then came right back.

"They're afraid to make it. They'll let you make it."

So Gabler and Holiday arranged that she and her Café Society band would cut "Strange Fruit" and three other numbers: "Yesterdays," "Fine and Mellow," and "I Gotta Right to Sing the Blues." Each song shows the second Holiday to perfection. "I Gotta Right" shows her Armstrongian roots as strongly as any song in her canon. Six years earlier, Armstrong (in the company of twenty-one-year-old Teddy Wilson) had made an eloquent revision of the Harold Arlen song for Victor Records. Holiday's remake is just as sprightly in its inventiveness and percussive impulse. The difference in mood, however, sets her apart from both Armstrong and the earlier Billie Holiday. A more despairing wail accompanies her treatment of the lyrics: "Soon the deep blue sea/Will be calling me." More darkness and tragedy sound through her "There's nothing left for me/I'm full of misery." It is easy to believe the truth in her drumming out of the words: "a certain man in this old town/…dragging my poor heart around./All I see for me is misery." Despite the fact that this song was made to order for juke joint and jukebox dancers, the tragic tone—beyond what people came to expect from the first Holiday—is palpable. It is as if the somber mood of "Strange Fruit" settled over the entire session, giving it a tragic dimension that was not present in her previous singing. This new dimension was present, too, in the subsequent Commodore session five years later. While she was fully capable of the joyous "Sunny Side of the Street," also recorded on that day, the main mode was slow and coolly detached in its sorrow. "How Am I to Know?" "My Old Flame," "I'll Get By," "I Cover the Waterfront," and "Embraceable You" all are in this new key of dramatically enacted sadness.

In the late 1930s, Holiday became close friends with one of her neighbors, Carmen McRae, who later became a premier jazz singer somewhat in the Holiday style. In 1936, before they met, fourteen-year-old McRae skipped school to sneak over to the Apollo where Holiday, whose records she admired,

was performing. In an interview in 1990, McRae recalled the first time she saw
the woman who became her idol:

Holiday with Joe Guy at the
Plantation Club on Central Avenue
in Los Angeles, c. 1945. Guy was
her lead trumpeter and escort—they
often introduced themselves as
husband and wife.

> *I stayed in the theater from the first show 'til the last. And I was just
> hypnotized sitting there looking at this woman. And I said, I just don't
> believe her. I thought she was extremely modern, you know. And she was
> kind of plump, but* sexy *looking, you know…. It was her left hand, I
> think: she held it up like this, and one hand was like this. And she never
> changed that position…. And she smiled a lot. And she was* beautiful.
> *What a beautiful, beautiful, beautiful woman. And all that engulfed
> me….. At first, when I first started to sing, I wanted to sound like her.*

McRae got the chance to meet Holiday through her friend Irene Kitchings.
McRae was a fledgling pianist who liked to sing and write songs. She was
seventeen when she played one of them, "Dream of Life," for Holiday, who
thrilled the talented teenager by deciding on the spot that she wanted to record
it. "Dream of Life" is a hauntingly beautiful composition, among those second
Holiday works that Michael Brooks has called "one of those brooding…pieces
Billie did so well, yet which died in the hands of other singers." The song's
rhythm section–driven beat is danceably steady, and the lyrics are hopeful, but
it is a second Holiday song because the melody is so unusual in its turns and
so darkly compelling.

In this same genre came four songs by Irene Kitchings (lyrics by Arthur
Hertzog): "Some Other Spring," "Ghost of Yesterday," "What Is This Going to
Get Us?" and "I'm Pulling Through." All of these are unusual and hauntingly
poignant pieces. The classic side is "Some Other Spring," written, McRae said
(like most of Kitchings's songs), in memory of "Ted," who had met someone
else and left her behind.

Holiday took "Some Other Spring" to Benny Goodman, who, she said,
thought "it was too beautiful, it wouldn't sell." She went ahead and recorded it
anyway. "He was right," she said. "It didn't sell." But the subtle beauty of the
melody and the poetry of the lyrics caused Michael Brooks to wonder what
happened to this team of songwriters: "There is just so much to ingest in the
words and music that it should be taken in small doses, like fine liquor brandy.
But oh, what poetry!" In this same vein are "Gloomy Sunday," "Deep Song,"
"God Bless the Child," "My Man," "Crazy He Calls Me," "Don't Explain,"
and "I Wonder Where Our Love Has Gone"—all declamatory songs in which

Holiday the dramatist and poet comes boldly forward working roots and magic. Holiday infused these torch songs with the sense of tragedy described by poet Gayle Jones, whose "Deep Song, For B.H." says starkly:

> *The blues calling my name*
> *She is singing a deep song.*
> *She is singing a deep song.*
> *I am human.*
> *He calls me crazy.*
> *He says, "You must be*
> *crazy."*
> *I say, "Yes, I'm crazy."…*
> *He is a dark man.*
> *Sometimes he is a good dark man.*
> *Sometimes he is a bad dark man.*
> *I love him.*

In these deep songs, where pain meets pleasure, Holiday sings of an inescapably tragic sense of life. She claims them, too, as part of the complex territory of her art. Who owned them is proved by the fact that almost no one else dares to sing them.

This second period was also the time when Holiday managed to hit the pay dirt of the mass market. To her credit, she did so, whether she used an orchestra of strings or not, without compromising her art, her true "story." Again she was working with Milt Gabler, who was now a pop artist and repertoire (A & R) man at Decca Records. Six nonjazz violins were used for "Lover Man" (1944), which inaugurated her six-year relationship with Decca and became her biggest-selling record of all time, but the arrangement is tasteful and unobtrusive, and her own vocal is nuanced and expressive. "Good Morning, Heartache," "Them There Eyes," "I Loves You, Porgy," "You're My Thrill," "Crazy He Calls Me," and "There Is No Greater Love" are vintage Holiday songs from this rich Decca era. I would single out "There Is No Greater Love," not the best known of this crossover cluster, as a masterwork worth discovering or rediscovering. Using the gifts described in Part I, she serves up the song with a lyricism seasoned and cooked down with gritty realism. She may have sung the same words that, say, Ella Fitzgerald sang when she delivered that pop tune, but she does so with the funereal slowness typical of this second period:

At the Downbeat Club in New York, 1946, Holiday performs with Lloyd Trotman, Tiny Grimes, Joe Guy (obscured), and Joe Springer.

(facing page)

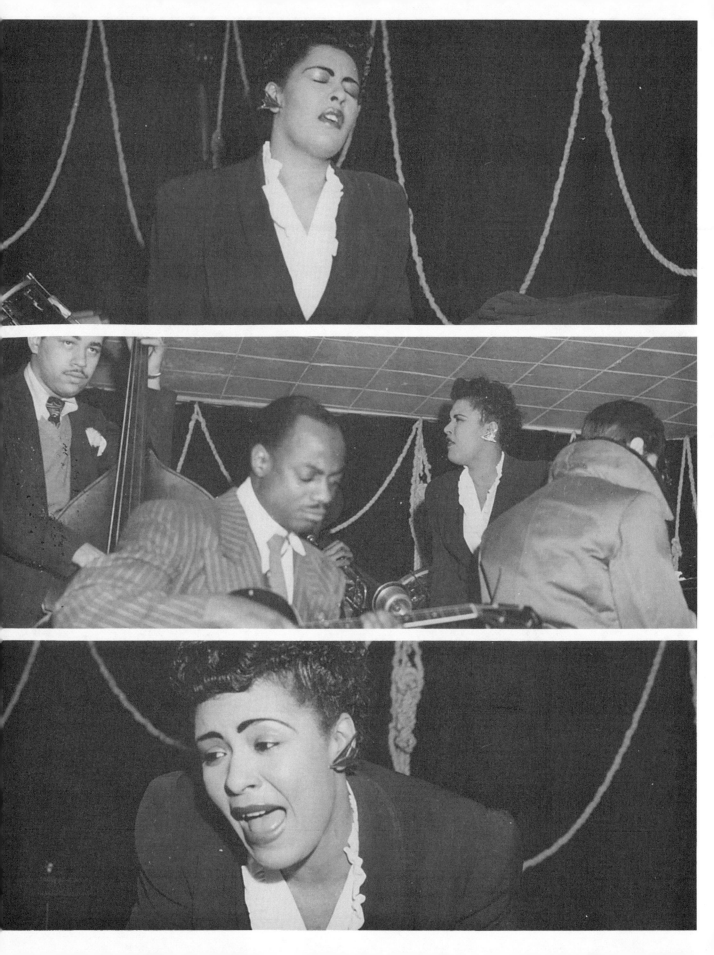

There is no greater love than what I feel for you,
No greater love,
No heart so true.

And her voice contains elements of anger and despair that at first seem unexpressed in the lyrics. When she sings the words "feeeel for you," she hits a low, low note, a rumbled D, at the very bottom of her range. And at that point, she seems to growl at her lover with something more than sensual allure and responsiveness. "There is no greater love" becomes a charge of unreciprocated love and enforced loneliness in a cosmos where "what I feel for you" is all the love there is and there is nothing greater. No wonder the poet Amiri Baraka said of Holiday, "Sometimes you are afraid to listen to this Lady." She crossed over, but she was never a smashing success because she did so without compromising the hard poetry of her deepest song.

In 1947, she appeared in a horrendous movie titled *New Orleans.* The film began as a serious effort to portray the cradle city of jazz in a way that worked as a visual story line but that also was analytical and true to the music. It ended as a silly collection of cardboard types, with Holiday (the woman who had said she never wanted to be "nobody's damn maid") cast as a singing maid. "She wasn't that great," said Carmen McRae. "Not that she had any good lines to say. She was *Lady!* The most unlikeliest person to be a maid to *anybody.*" Still, despite everything (for example, the decision that during Lady Day's big nightclub number, it would be a good idea to superimpose footage of a train barreling through Holiday's face), somehow the music has persevered. True to a long tradition of black artists in American films, Holiday, with her slyly subversive eyes, takes over the movie when at last it gives the audience a chance to see her (with Louis Armstrong) in song, telling her story. Her versions of "The Blues Are Brewin'" and "New Orleans" will last when the rest of the movie is justly forgotten.

One last feature of this second Holiday stands out: the truly outstanding singer of both blues and near-blues. (I use "near-blues" to describe songs such as "Pigfoot and a Bottle of Beer," which is not set in a twelve-bar blues form but uses virtually all the other musical elements of the blues.) In some ways, it is the most appealing feature of the period. As I have emphasized, Holiday was not primarily a blues singer, but do not forget that she started out imitating Bessie Smith, who was a blues diva of the highest power, and that Louis Armstrong, who was if anything even more of an influence on Holiday than was Smith, also

Holiday at New York's Metropolitan Opera House during a 1944 performance with Art Tatum, Big Sid Catlett, and Jack Teagarden, winners of *Esquire*'s first jazz critics' poll. (below)

was an extraordinarily capable exponent of the down-home blues. Her first blues recording was "Big City Blues (The Saddest Tale)" of 1935. The next one, "Billie's Blues" (1936), did not come until twenty-two pop and show songs had intervened. Both evoked the memory of Armstrong and Smith. Both also had a modern swing and lilt to them, and both offered an eloquent interpretation of the lyrics that went beyond what either Smith or Armstrong attempted in their blues. Holiday's next blues were the wonderful "Long Gone Blues" and "Fine and Mellow" (1939); "St. Louis Blues" and "Loveless Love" (1940); and "I Love My Man (Billie's Blues)" (1944). She released more blues songs in the late forties and fifties.

Regarding the blues (and the near-blues) of the second Holiday, the most arresting development was her apparent effort to put together a series of songs in tribute to Bessie Smith. Between 1940 and 1949, Holiday recorded six songs previously recorded by Smith: "St. Louis Blues," "Careless Love" (or its variant, "Loveless Love"), "Ain't Nobody's Business," "Keeps on A-Rainin'," "Do Your Duty," and "Gimme a Pigfoot." Milt Gabler remembered no systematically pursued "Billie Sings Bessie" project, but the fact that Holiday recorded four of these Smith songs in a three-week period makes clear that some kind of Holiday-Smith series was on somebody's mind. It is also notable that two of these songs came from Smith's final recording session—the one in which she said she did not want to make any more blues records but instead preferred to record songs that were more modern: "something in a jazz vein."

Perhaps all that need be said here is that taken together, both Smith's originals and Holiday's remakes are magnificent examples of the idiom. Who would be so headstrong as to keep one singer's versions of the songs and to throw away the others? Take the case of "Pigfoot and a Bottle of Beer." Smith sings it starting with her huge roadhouse-woman's voice, saying, "Twenty-five cents?! No, no, I ain't paying twenty-five cents to go in *nowhere*." From these opening lines on, she seems to own the song forever. Her voice broadcasts like a boldly ragged "talking" New Orleans trombone and captures the sense of predawn revelry and barely contained chaos of the night-town moment when "Old Hanna Brown from 'cross town/ Gets full of corn and starts breakin' 'em down." It's here, in Smith's voice, that an "all-night strut…up in Harlem on a Saturday night" in the 1930s meets and merges with a juke house session in Chattanooga, Tennessee, of the late nineteenth century—where and when this marvelous singer entered the world. It does not seem possible to add anything to this definitive statement of the song. And yet Holiday's version of 1949 also is definitive. The fourteen-piece orchestra is a studio unit consisting of Buck Clayton and sax giant Budd Johnson, with Sy Oliver arranging and conducting. Oliver was a veteran trumpeter and singer of Jimmy Lunceford's jumping band of the mid- to late thirties. In fact, during his Lunceford years, Oliver was the arranger usually credited with creating what was known as the Lunceford style. What Leonard Feather wrote about his arranging in general is quite true of Holiday's "Pigfoot" arrangement in particular: "Oliver's writing made use of many simple, swinging effects, frequent staccato phrases that often had a touch of humor, and a brilliant sense of continuity and climax."

By 1949, Smith's influence on Holiday seemed academic; Holiday was no longer one of Smith's (or Armstrong's) children. She had taken what she needed from her "artistic parents" and had become, so to speak, *her own daughter*. She never attained "Bessie's big sound" (her name for what she wanted most from Smith), but she did learn to tell her own story with what sound she did command and to master what she wanted of Smith's turns of note and phrase. In the case of "Pigfoot," Holiday tore out a page from Smith's songbook and pasted it

Photos taken on the set of the movie *New Orleans* in 1946. From left to right: Louis Armstrong, Charlie Beal, Holiday, Kid Ory (back to camera), Barney Bigard, and Bud Scott. (top, facing page)

With the movie's "star," Dorothy Patrick. (bottom, facing page)

boldly into her own. She riffs on the song, Armstrong style, and gives it her characteristic pace, sauciness, and dramatic vividness. In her "Pigfoot," what "they do" on Saturday night in Harlem is not "Tut-tut-tut" (as Smith says), it is brazenly "Ooo-papa-dop." Holiday's "Pigfoot" is a distinctively urban (as opposed to Smith's down-home rural) trotter; it is a "good foot" highly seasoned with deep southern blues but also with the kind of blues the beboppers blew. Still, Holiday's excursions back into the blues are praise songs for Smith and Armstrong and for the blues as a vital tradition and source. Harking back to this music's history and simultaneously pushing it forward, Holiday's blues speak for those generations of listeners/dancers who knew the trouble she had seen and who nonetheless sang with her the aggressively defiant "Glory Hallelujah" that gives the blues its testamental power of transcendence. More than Smith's blues, Holiday's see trouble everywhere but proclaim that she (and therefore we) can live through it.

"I opened Café Society as an unknown," Holiday said. "I left two years later as a star." From the Café Society, she went to the jazz clubs of southern

California, where she played white clubs and mixed after-hours joints, meeting Hollywood luminaries and underworld figures along the way. Back in New York in 1942, she played the Famous Door on Fifty-second Street and began the climb from one hundred dollars a week, her first salary at the Famous Door, to one thousand and then two thousand dollars a week by the end of the decade. In small clubs in brownstones along Swing Street, known among jazz players and aficionados simply as "The Street," Holiday appeared with Art Tatum, Coleman Hawkins, Roy Eldridge, Lester Young, Nat "King" Cole, and others. And even though The Street's segregation policy meant that in its early days only whites were admitted into its basement hideaways (Holiday called working The Street "working on a plantation"), eventually the separatist policies broke down. Even in the worst days, as far as integration was concerned, Holiday's career was on the way up. She noted, "Working on the street seemed like a homecoming every night. People I'd met in Harlem, Hollywood, and Café Society used to come in and there was always some kind of reunion. I was getting a little billing and publicity, so my old friends and acquaintances knew where to find me."

Standing at kissing distance from fellow musicians and audiences alike, Holiday ruled The Street's music scene. Many people have reported going night after night to see her now magisterial Lady Day entrance—sometimes with one

Left to right: Holiday backstage with Jimmy Mundy, Robert Scott, and Gene Ammons, c. 1946. (overleaf)

Holiday looked anxious joining this group between sets at a club, c. 1948. Second from right is her pianist, Bobby Tucker.

Barred from New York's nightclubs, Holiday opened on Broadway in 1948. After opening acts by Slam Stewart and Cozy Cole, Holiday and her band, featuring Bobby Tucker on piano, did their regular club routine on the broad stage of the Mansfield Theater. The show received fairly good reviews but closed after just three weeks, and Holiday was back to playing one-nighters and, at best, gigs that lasted for a few weeks each.

or two dogs in tow—and to wait for the moment when she would appear before them to tell her musical stories. She would give "Strange Fruit" or "Some Other Spring" style recitatives, or, as she had done all her life, she would swing Swing Street off its fancy hinges with a jump tune from down in Baltimore or up in Harlem.

Teddy Wilson told an interviewer that in 1941, near the start of Holiday's second stage, she came to see him at a midtown club and said that at last she felt that she had discovered her own artistic voice. "She told me that she'd really found herself as a singer—whereas everyone else felt that she had found herself before. But a person doesn't always hear herself as others do. She was singing very much to her personal satisfaction in 1941. She was beginning to hear herself." By 1949, she was a thoroughly seasoned artist, very much in control of her powers and possibilities. The stage was set for the third Holiday, the controversial Lady of her last ten years.

•   •   •

The third Holiday is the Billie Holiday with verve—verve both in the sense of Lady Day's supreme vitality, to the last, and in that she was recording almost exclusively for the California-based label called Clef and then Verve.

As we have seen, Milt Gabler, Holiday's associate from the days of the Commodore Record Store and the Commodore label, had been her A & R man at Decca and had been crucial to the responsible management of her crossover efforts. But in 1950, a shake-up at Decca took Gabler off the jazz beat, and Holiday was set adrift. Aside from air checks and bootleg sessions— and a so-so session at Alladin Records that was almost completely undermined by the foghorn saxophoning of Haywood Henry—Holiday made no records from March 1950, when the Decca deal ran out, until March 1952, when she signed with Verve. During the Verve years, 1952 to 1957, Holiday did four ten-inch albums and seventeen twelve-inch albums—more than a hundred songs in all. (For discographers, the picture is complicated by Verve's 1985 release of a "live" Holiday session at Carnegie Hall in 1947.)

Aside from the Verves, Holiday made two other great recordings during this last period. They are "Fine and Mellow," her appearance on the television special "The Sound of Jazz," and *Lady in Satin,* her penultimate album, done for Columbia. The standard line on these last dates is that they are not very good, that she was so strung out on heroin and so torn to pieces by hard living

Holiday at Town Hall in New York, 1946. With Holiday are Tiny Grimes (guitar), Lloyd Trotman (bass), and Joe Guy (trumpet).

While on the road, Holiday, out of money, wrote this letter to her agent, Joe Glaser. (facing page)

that she was little more than a self-parody. Most serious commentary on her work steers listeners back to the "golden" days of the thirties, when she was the girl with the silvery sparkle in her voice. Notice that Time-Life's "Giants of Jazz" collection — so dependable in most instances — follows the party line and selects for the Billie Holiday box only songs prior to 1946; of the forty songs selected, thirty-six are from the thirties. Likewise, for the Book-of-the-Month-Club box, Nat Hentoff chose nothing at all from the Verve catalog. (He did pick two pieces from the fifties.)

Part of what gives here is the myth of the "natural" artist. It is the pastoral fallacy at work, the idea that artists are by definition at their best when they are the least schooled. Recall John Hammond's objection to the Holiday of "Strange Fruit" (1939) and beyond: she was too arty, too self-consciously mannered. Note again, in contrast, her own statement to Teddy Wilson that at about that time, she felt that she had finally begun to discover herself as a singer. By the fifties, Hammond and many others had given up on Holiday. She was no longer the fresh original; maybe because of drugs, some have said, she stooped to the point of imitating herself.

This is nonsense. It is certainly true that the voice of the third Holiday had lost some of its youthful push and radiancy. It is also true that on off nights in the fifties, for the first time she could be wretchedly off. At times she seemed too weak physically and too poor in spirit to give the world yet another song. But until the last months of her life (when she began to decline at a fiercely rapid pace and probably should not have been out of her sickbed, much less performing), the off nights were exceedingly rare. Elizabeth Hardwick saw Holiday during those years of decidedly less consistent exuberance. Hardwick's account of Holiday getting through yet another evening is eloquent and disquieting:

She was always behind a closed door — the fate of those addicted to whatever. And then at last she must come forward, emerge in powders and Vaseline, hair twisted with a curling iron, gloves of satin or silk jersey, flowers — the expensive martyrdom of the "entertainer".

At that time not so many of her records were in print and she was seldom heard on the radio because her voice did not accord with popular taste then. The appearances in night clubs were a necessity. It was a burden to be there night after night, although not a burden to sing, once she had started, in her own way. She knew she could do

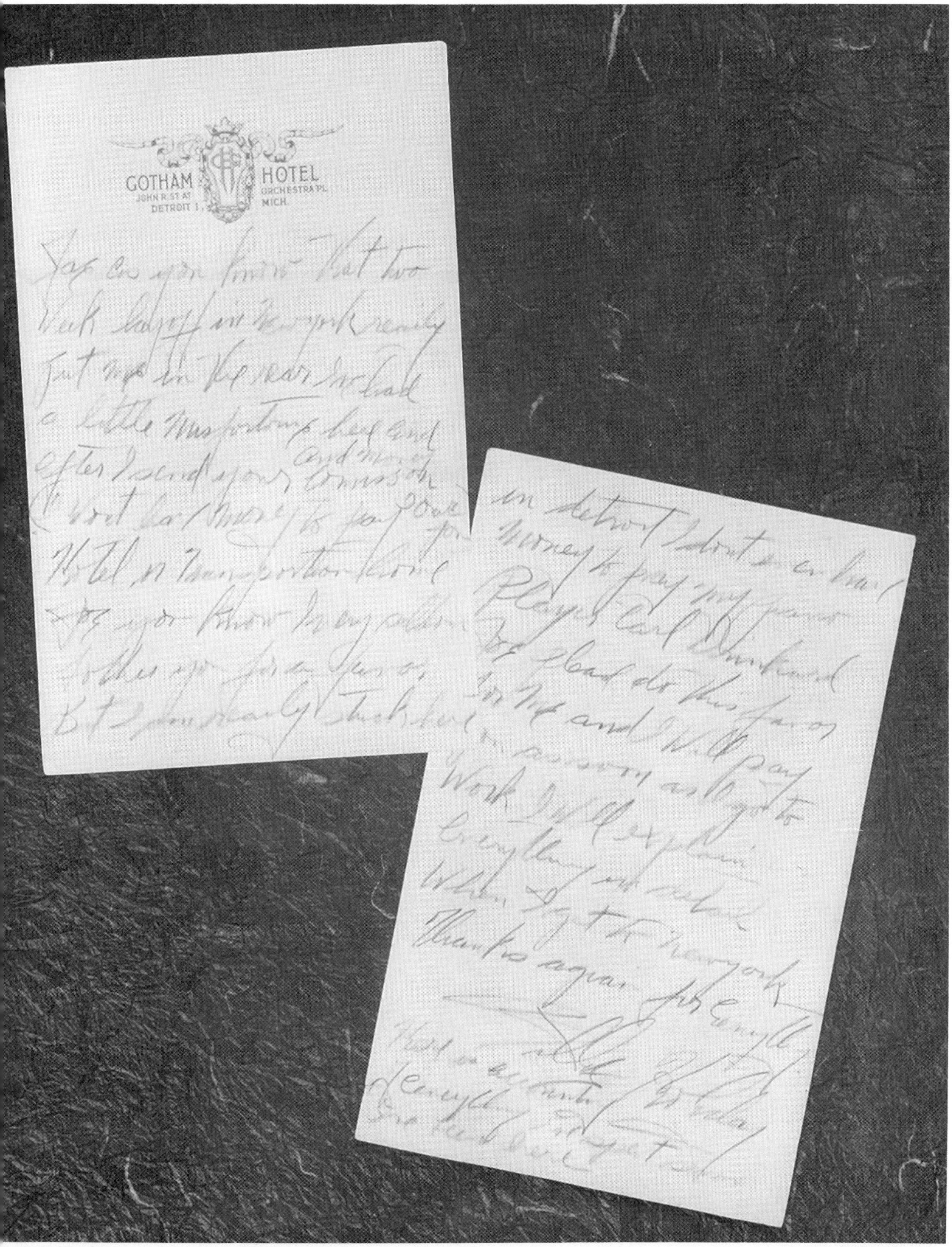

GOTHAM HOTEL
JOHN R. ST. AT
DETROIT 1,
ORCHESTRA PL.
MICH.

As you know that two
week layoff in New York nearly
put me in the rear, I had
a little misfortune here and
after I send you commission
and money I won't have money to pay our
Hotel or Transportation home
as you know we only played
in Detroit you for a few os,
but I am nearly stuck here

in Detroit I don't have
money to pay my piano
player Carl Armhard
so please do this favor
for me and I will pay
you as soon as I get to
work I will explain
everything in detail
when I get to New York
Thanks again for Everything
Best to everybody
if everything
go well here I expect to arrive

it, that she had mastered it all, but why not ask the question: Is this all there is? Her work took on, gradually, a destructive cast, as it so often does with the greatly gifted who are doomed to repeat endlessly their own heights of inspiration....

Her whole life had taken place in the dark. The spotlight shone down on the black, hushed circle in a café; the moon slowly slid through the clouds. Night-working, smiling, in make-up, in long, silky dresses, singing over and over, again and again. The aim of it all is just to be drifting off to sleep when the first rays of the sun's brightness threaten the theatrical eyelids.

Holiday with Lester Young, c. 1950.

All the same, it is true that in this last period of the third Holiday, she operated in surly defiance of the destructive downspin of her situation. And contrary to the pastoral myth that less is somehow more and more somehow less, Holiday kept right on evolving as an artist. When she was at her very best, which was often, she was an even greater artist than she had ever been before. By the mid-fifties, her vocal equipment was weaker but her style was entirely her own and her musical techniques—her playful sense of timing, her subtly nuanced phrasing, her control of tonal color, her capacity to reinvent songs— were more advanced than ever before. Despite the nightmarish world of trouble through which she moved, Holiday was singing better than ever.

Nowhere is this fact more evident than in her 1952 remake of "These Foolish Things," which she had first recorded in 1936. Martin Williams, who chose the 1952 version for the boxed set *The Smithsonian Collection of Classic Jazz* (no doubt the most influential of all the boxes I have mentioned), observes that in 1952 Holiday made ingenious revisions of both the songwriter's original tune and her own sensational 1936 recomposition of it. Of the 1952 "These Foolish Things," Williams aptly notes:

Holiday, c. 1945. Between shows, Holiday obliges a photographer with a shot of her with an unknown performer, perhaps in a comedy or "jungle" skit.

She retains the original song's best melodic phrases, but instinctively rejects its inferior ones, filling in with new melodic lines of her own that are more interesting and more appropriate. In her earlier version of "These Foolish Things" she had similarly spotted its inferior moments but she was still a bit intimidated by them, and rather than come up with new melodic phrases of her own she had used simple blues devices to avoid them.

Holiday at the start of her European tour, 1954. Left to right: Buddy DeFranco, Red Norvo, Beryl Booker, Leonard Feather, Holiday, and Louis McKay.

Writing elsewhere of the 1952 version of the song, he continues his analysis: "The reading here is superior in almost every way, and although Holiday's vocal instrument had deteriorated, her musicianship had grown greatly. She is very well aware of the harmonic structure of the piece, and she virtually re-writes the song's A section [see Figure 1] into a deceptively complex melody of her own."

Original melody

Billie Holiday's version

(Figure 1)

What makes the third Holiday so great is precisely that she did seem to know just what she ought to keep and what she ought to alter or erase. She had spent her career recomposing Gershwin, Arlen, Ellington, and far lesser lights; now she had taken to recomposing Billie Holiday as well. She knew that there was much to retain of the earlier Holiday. Like the Holiday Columbias with Teddy Wilson, the Holiday Verves use no tightly set arrangements of strings or horns. Rather, they retain the earlier period's jam session–chamber music spirit in which the hallmarks are great rhythm underlying great conversational interplay among musicians, including Holiday. For rhythm, Verve's owner and artistic director, Norman Granz, used Verve regulars, including the outstanding Oscar Peterson–led trios or quartets, or studio groups involving other superb pianists such as Jimmy Rowles, Bobby Tucker, and Wynton Kelly. The horn players, many of whom had been contributors to Holiday sessions in the thirties, represent a Who's Who of jazz horns. Alternating on saxes were Ben Webster, Benny Carter, Coleman Hawkins, Budd Johnson, Flip Philips, Willie Smith, and Paul Quinichette (the man called "Vice Prez" in honor of his affinity to Lester Young). The featured trumpet player was Harry "Sweets" Edison, who alternated with Charlie Shavers or Joe Newman, also excellent players. For these

Verve sessions, as for the earliest Columbia ones, Holiday and the piano player (or a nominal leader designated by Granz) would sketch out minimal opening and closing figures. Sometimes to the chagrin of the artists (Jimmy Rowles always complained that he was playing great but could never get any awards because he never got to play enough solos), Granz would set the solo sequences. Granz and Holiday agreed that these new records should retain the excitement of the unimpeded improvisation that had made the thirties material classic. And although her musical conversations with Ben Webster in particular, but also with Edison and Carter, are usually overlooked, they are as wonderful as any duets with horns that she ever put on record. They rank even among the Holiday-Young masterpieces of the 1930s. What could be finer than the Holiday-Webster work on "I Didn't Know What Time It Was," "Our Love Is Here to Stay," and "We'll Be Together Again"?

There are finger-popping dance tunes in this Verve catalog, too. Holiday's "Day In, Day Out," "Comes Love," and "Please Don't Talk about Me When I'm Gone" seem made for the jukebox, the dance floor, or the house party with the coffee table pushed to the corner. But by the fifties, Holiday had established herself—in part because of the "Strange Fruit" style songs—as a mood singer, an artist to enjoy while relaxing between dances. "You Go to My Head," "Solitude," "Willow Weep For Me" (the Newport version), and "Do Nothing 'Til You Hear from Me" are magnificent ballads that Holiday delivers with supreme control

and concentration. She is not sifting through Tin Pan Alley song sheets for a song she can redeem here. She is doing the American songbook's finest, most difficult songs, such as "Prelude to a Kiss" and "I Don't Want to Cry Anymore." In a taped rehearsal with Jimmy Rowles and Artie Shapiro, 1955, Holiday goes over songs for an upcoming Verve session. The most fascinating thing about that candid recording is that it shows that she was the boss of the trio, she was the one setting the songs' moods, keys, and arrangements. When they rehearse "I Don't Want to Cry Anymore," she consoles Rowles, "You only got one little part that's kind of puzzling you. This is *hard*, Jack. This is a hard tune. That's why don't nobody fuck with it." Then they go over it again.

In virtually every case, the Verve remake of a song she recorded before is better than the earlier version. In "My Man," "Don't Explain," and "Body and Soul," her lower, raspier, and wiser voice gives the song more resonance and depth. In 1958, Miles Davis told Nat Hentoff, "You know, she's not thinking now what she was in 1937, and she's probably learned more about different things. And she still has control, probably more control now than then. No, I don't think she's in a decline. A lot of singers try to sing like Billie, but just the act of playing behind the beat doesn't make it sound soulful."

Throughout the Verves, Holiday pruned away every superficiality. Like late Armstrong, the third Holiday retains the soul of the music without offering the consolation of sentimentality or needless decoration. Explaining to Jimmy Rowles how she wants to do "Everything Happens to Me," she says, "Hey baby, you know how I want to do this? Everybody has did it sooo pretty, I want to do it [she snaps her fingers to set the tempo and then sings] *Ahhh-doowee-dowee-dow and real funky-funky and I mean, I want the people to know just what I'm talking about....* There you go." Her later version is earthy and rich. The young girl's clear-toned yearning is gone. In its place is the voice of the boss of the band and a rich palette of tragic colors.

For the album *Lady in Satin* (1958), Holiday wanted sections of strings and jazz horns. The result is mixed. Ray Ellis's arrangements are caressing but sometimes flaccid, and Holiday's voice sounds ravaged in places and uncertain. Yet on the whole, the smooth strings provide a fascinating contrast to the roughness of Holiday's sound, and a few songs from that album—"You've Changed," "I'm a Fool to Want You," and "I Get Along without You Very Well"—are priceless third Holiday. Annie Ross, the singer most famous for her association with Lambert, Hendricks, and Ross, remembered Holiday's work on *Lady in Satin:* "Her voice had an intimacy. You felt she had lived through the

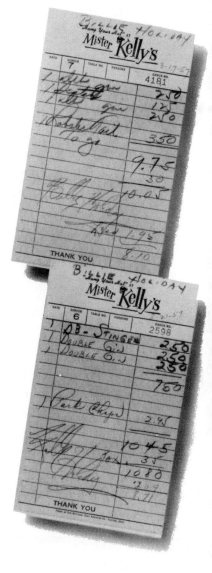

Holiday in Chicago, 1957. Holiday loved lobster and pork chops. Between shows, she would have them sent to her dressing room with a double gin or vodka.

lyrics she was singing; she knew what she was singing about. And she also had that kind of thing they call charisma, I guess: that thing that makes you think she's singing only to you…. She had *soul*. I mean, even an album like *Lady in Satin*, where people say 'Oh, the *voice* is gone.' Not for me. There's a whole *life* in that voice."

And Carmen McRae assessed *Lady in Satin* this way:

> *Her voice wasn't anywhere near where it had been. But boy, I still listen to that. I have three of those albums, because I don't want to wear them out. I cry. I listen to "I'm a Fool to Want You" and ohhhhhh, it breaks my heart. And I just say, "Sing it Lady." And her voice wasn't what it had been, we know that. But it was so effective. It was much more effective then, to me, than when it was in great shape…. She had the heart and the soul. And she had stuff to do to make you cry, and…hey, who could ask for anything more?*

Moving from city to city, usually with just her pianist (the rest of the band would be picked from among local musicians), Holiday performed her best-known numbers. Before going on, she and the piano player worked out the order of the songs. This set list, c. 1957, is in her handwriting and probably was balanced on the piano so that both she and the piano player could see it and know what was coming next. Once the show was on, she would alter the selections of songs if her mood shifted or the feeling she got from the audience called for something different.

The year before, in 1957, Holiday had taken part in the best short film in the history of jazz cinematography. Strictly speaking, it is not a film at all but a recorded television program, now issued in its entirety as a videocassette tape titled "The Sound of Jazz." In it Holiday performs "Fine and Mellow" accompanied by an all-star group of jazz players, some of whom she had been making records with for more than twenty years. The lineup is out of a dream: Lester Young, Ben Webster, Coleman Hawkins, and Gerry Mulligan (saxes); Roy Eldridge and Doc Cheatham (trumpets); Vic Dickenson (trombone); Mal Waldron (piano); Danny Barker (guitar); Milt Hinton (bass); Osie Johnson (drums). Holiday and Young had become estranged somehow, but soon afterward Young told an interviewer that she was still his favorite singer: "She's still my Lady Day." He was so weak and sick that he had to sit down and gather his strength while the band played "Fine and Mellow." On film he stands up just long enough to take a brief solo. Nat Hentoff, Whitney Balliett, and producer Robert Herridge had put the program together. Hentoff's eloquent description of Young's solo are now part of the scene's memory:

> *He blew the sparest, purest blues I had ever heard. Billie, smiling, nodding to the beat, looked into Prez's eyes and he into hers. She was looking back with the gentlest of regrets at their past. Prez was remembering too. Whatever had blighted their relationship was*

*forgotten in the communion of the music. Sitting in the control room
I felt tears, and saw tears in the eyes of most of the others there. The
rest of the program was all right, but this had been its climax — the
empirical soul of jazz.*

After Young's remarkable solo, Holiday comes back in with "He wears
high draped pants/Stripes are really yellow." One marvels again at how close
her voice is to Young's instrument: her hornlike voice, his voicelike horn — the

Holiday and Lester Young, 1957.

most perfectly matched instruments in jazz. As we listen to her match solos with Hawkins, Webster, Eldridge, and the rest, it is never more clear that hers was one of this century's most evocative voices, in or out of jazz.

"Fine and Mellow" is a blues song, not a protest song. But like other great blues songs, it offers an implied protest against human shortcomings—in this case, against the failure of love to be enduring and unambiguous. It also seems to speak to social issues of the time. Coming precisely at the moment when the civil rights movement was taking off, this filmed version of the song reminds us of the strained relations between blacks and whites in Little Rock, Arkansas, and all over the nation. Holiday addresses the song to her disappointing man in "high draped pants," but she could be speaking to white America at large:

> *Love is just like a faucet;*
> *It turns off and on.*
> *Love is like a faucet;*
> *It turns off and on.*
> *Sometimes when you thinks it's on, baby;*
> *It has turned off and gone.*

It is no wonder that Albert Murray has said that the blues could serve as America's national anthem. They are as close as we can stand to get to tragedy, writes Ralph Ellison. Murray reminds us that blues music and the best of its makers celebrate our finest features as Americans (not so evident in 1957 or, for that matter, in 1991)—individuality as well as group consciousness; cool hardiness under pressure; and the ability, as we face troubles, to show resiliency and steadfastness as we improvise on changes. These ideals are expressed in this music much better than in any other place. If "Fine and Mellow" is our anthem, then this 1957 rendition is the unsurpassed version of it. As a movie, it offers images of equality: across lines of gender, age, and race, these musicians make meaningful music together. "Fine and Mellow" is third Holiday at its best.

Ben Webster, c. 1951. Webster's sound had a mature, burnished quality, much like Holiday's. Holiday cut her first Holiday-Wilson records of 1935—and several other subsequent ones of that early period—with Webster as a key sideman. He surfaced again in the fifties as the leading horn on her masterpieces for Verve Records, where many of the most alluring of her dark arias feature his accompaniment.

Part Five

· · ·

LADY AT THE MET

This book argues that the most convenient escape from the
difficulty of confronting the meaning of Billie Holiday's life
is the assertion that she was not a cultivated artist but a
natural. Well-intentioned friends of blacks and women point
to her story as the apotheosis of the victim's tale. Seen in this
way, the incantatory recital of her woes — her teenage parents,
her father's desertion, her experiences of prostitution and rape, her exploitive
lover/managers, her use of dope and criminal record, the loss of her cabaret
license, her color and sex — seems to help explain why "Lady sang the blues"
so convincingly. Not a blues singer? Many critics have told us that even when
she sang nonblues songs, she turned them into the blues: she blued them with
her natural blues voice born of blues living.

Some commentators have cringed at the unpleasant facts of her life, as if
they were unspeakable or some sort of betrayal. To a degree, these writers' distaste
for lived complexity or contradiction, especially when it surfaces in women or
blacks, colors their interpretations. Here was an African American woman whose
piano player, Bobby Tucker, described as having "the *most* terrible inferiority
complex." She "actually doesn't believe she can sing," he said. Yet somehow this
same woman, at eighteen, was trading choruses with some of the greatest jazz
players in the world. By the time she was twenty-one, she had sung with Duke
Ellington's orchestra in a movie and was a headliner with Count Basie at the
Savoy Ballroom on the night when many people present said she and the band
outperformed Ella Fitzgerald and the mythically unsurpassable "Savoy King,"
Chick Webb. When club owners told her to change her way of singing, she

would throw things, cuss them out, and change nothing. She would quit first, as she did more than once. When the audience at the Café Society seemed too inattentive to her rendition of "Strange Fruit," she broke off the song and walked off, pausing just long enough to flip up her gown and show her naked behind to the silenced hordes.

This woman, who was decidedly not a member of the Cult of True Womanhood — that nineteenth-century mythic construct that posited the cardinal virtues for the "true woman" as "piety, purity, submissiveness, and domesticity" — did feel pressured to conform to "true woman" rules. Memry Midgett, Holiday's friend and occasional piano player in the 1950s, told an interviewer that the singer sometimes would call her long distance in the middle of the night, worried about the state of her soul. Frequently in the press, Holiday would claim to be settling down: "I just want to be a housewife," she told a *Down Beat* writer in 1957, "and take care of Mr. McKay." Louis McKay, her last husband, served as a consultant to the Hollywood film *Lady Sings the Blues,* and it is telling that the filmmakers put together an extraordinarily attractive part for the actor who played him (Billy Dee Williams). McKay took issue with those who said the film was too negative, grotesquely invoking the Cult values portrayed. "I really like the way it shows the relationship she and I had," he said. "Billie and I were very much in love although we had our problems…. She was much, much more

Holiday with daughters of friends in Oakland, California, 1950s. (left)

Holiday with Louis McKay. (right)

'All I Want Is to Sing—And Have a Baby'
Billie Holiday Says She's Paid Debt to Society, Is Set for Career

By WAMBLY BALD

"I guess I paid my dues to society," said Billie Holiday. "Maybe I overpaid. But now nuthin' is goin' to stop me. All I want now is to just sing—and have a baby."

After 10 months in a reformatory on a narcotics charge, the moan-voiced singer looked high-spirited and happy.

Her vitality dominated the office of Al Wilde, producer of the first full-length stage presentation in her career, opening at the Mansfield Tuesday. She has already made a jam-packed comeback at Carnegie Hall, 11 days after being released from the Federal Reformatory for Women at Alderson, W. Va.

"I ain't squawkin'," she said, "because nobody held a pistol to my head to make me use the stuff. I just got in with the wrong bunch, and pretty soon I got hooked, that's all. I learned my lesson."

The toughest part was abrupt deprivation of the "stuff" at the reformatory, she said.

"Hell couldn't be no worse. They didn't wean me off slow. I just had to kick it off cold tur-

BILLIE HOLIDAY
Paid her "dues"

key. But in 19 days I was back on my feet and out working on the farm. The doctors couldn't believe it!"

"I told them I wanted hard physical labor so's I could sleep nights. It was grand exercise but I put on 35 pounds. Too many starches. Too many potatoes and beans. Still, I feel good now."

Fan letters came to her from all over the world, she said, but she wasn't permitted to receive them until the day of her release.

"There are a lot of people in my corner now rooting for me," she added. "I won't let them down."

Miss Holiday is now making her home in Morristown, N. J. She lives with the family of her accompanist, Bobby Tucker.

"I bought a piece of land last week, and it's right next door to the Tuckers. It'll be my first own home, and do you know who'll be in it? My husband, Jimmie Monroe.

"We got separated three years ago, and he scrammed down to California," she said. "But he's just come back and looked me up, and we're going to be together, and we're to have a home and a baby and contentment. There's a lot more to life than getting high, and glamour."

than most people realize who saw her only as a glamorous star, then as someone caught up in the narcotics thing. She was a tender loving woman who liked nothing better than being at home with her man, cooking meals for me and doing little things around the house." (Memry Midgett often saw Holiday and McKay together and remembered him as a brutal "pimp" who was "one of the most ruthless men I have ever met. He exploited Billie Holiday completely," keeping her in dark rooms without adequate clothing and eating out of cans. Earl Zaidins, Holiday's lawyer, recalled letting her hide from McKay in the bathroom of his apartment after McKay had attacked her.)

One of Holiday's versions of her acceptance of the nickname "Lady" shows a degree of deference to the Cult of True Womanhood. Holiday admitted that she may have had to work for a living, and even to work in dives where she and singers like Detroit Red sang off-color tunes and pulled up their dresses to collect money between their legs. "But I didn't like the idea of showing my body," she said. "There was nothing wrong with my body, I just didn't like the idea." When a "millionaire" gave up on her clumsy efforts to take twenty dollars from his table, he first shooed her away and then invited her over for a drink. He gave her the money in her hand. "I figured, if a millionaire could give me money that way, everybody could. So from then on I wouldn't take money off tables. When I came to work the other girls used to razz me, call me 'Duchess' and say, 'Look at her, she thinks she's a lady.' I hadn't gotten my title Lady Day yet, but that was the beginning of people calling me 'Lady.'"

Black families sometimes raised their daughters to exhibit the Cult's virtues more than their white sisters. In this best-foot-forward tradition, Holiday's family never let her forget that she was a "bastard child" who needed to prove to the world that she had not inherited her mother's "scarlet letter." Her cousin John Fagan recalled that although all the Fagans now celebrate their famous relative, in the 1920s and 1930s, certain members of the Fagan clan, notably Holiday's formidable great-aunt Rosie Brooks, ceased speaking to or of Sadie Fagan once Billie (née Eleanora) was born out of wedlock. Naturally, Aunt Rosie had nothing whatsoever to do with Eleanora. In response to a mountain of family pressure, Sadie tried throughout her life to show that she was a respectable woman, a "true woman." She was a staunch Catholic and was a hardworking woman who

Holiday, late 1950s.

seems never to have been without a job. Those who knew them have said that Sadie and her daughter were "like sisters together." In part that meant they were forever at odds, with "older sister" Sadie warning Eleanora about the perils of slipping too far from Cult ideals.

Personal friends report that Sadie was immeasurably proud of her talented offspring but that she always criticized Eleanora's late hours and no-good friends— especially the men. In her autobiography, Holiday says that she set her mother up in business with a restaurant in New York. But one club owner reported that Holiday was so reticent about giving her mother financial help that he felt pressed into agreeing to give her regular stipends taken out of Holiday's pay, unbeknownst to the singer. From Sadie's point of view, the girl could sing, but she still had not learned how to behave. Eleanora was not at all willing to help her mother live down her bad reputation within the family. In the words of the black vernacular of the period, Eleanora just would not *do*. Concerning her childhood interest in Louis Armstrong and Bessie Smith, Holiday's report on her family's response is brief and quite significant: "Many's the whipping I got for listening to their records when I was a child."

As noted before, in Holiday's own recollection of her family history, her great-grandmother figures quite prominently. "She was ninety-six and I was six or seven. We really loved each other. She used to talk about how it felt to be a slave, about life, about all the stories in the Bible, everything." Of this woman, who seems to have been named Rebecca Fagan and who may have come from Virginia or West Virginia, we know next to nothing except what Holiday tells us. But the fact that Holiday felt so connected with her is quite significant, as is the fact that Holiday always believed that she had killed the old woman. She had forever cut herself off from this much-loved kindred spirit who, as a slave, knew what it meant to be trapped in a system where a black woman's market value was linked to the exploitability of her body and work. For her accidental "crime" against the grandmother and the family, Holiday's aunt gave her an unforgettable beating: "The doctor tried to stop her. He said if she didn't stop I'd grow up nervous. But she never stopped." This was bad Sadie's bad girl; she needed the devil beaten out of her.

Holiday grew up with a feeling of intense aloneness and guilt. She grew up acutely aware of the social standards from which she was at variance, and yet she flaunted that variance. Not just her family but many standard-bearers of the black community and women wished she would disappear. She was not a good girl; she was not a credit to "her people."

Holiday with Charlie Parker and an unknown youngster, c. 1953.

Holiday's angry letter to Tallulah Bankhead, a close acquaintance during the late 1940s. "Banky" did not wish to be mentioned in Holiday's autobiography—and threatened a suit if she was, presumably because Holiday was a known drug addict and the movie actress feared that the association would injure her career.

At the other extreme, some were put off by Holiday not because she was not a "true woman," but because she was too much of one. Despite her bold showings of contrariness and her achievements as an artist, she was suicidally submissive to men. She had been a girl prostitute. She was controlled by one entrepreneur/lover after another, by drugs, and by drug-dealing entrepreneur/lovers who pimped her talent. Because she had been an abused child who grew up with violence all around her, she was drawn to the panther-pretty men in her life, the most brutal ones she could find. That is why when she chose women lovers, she preferred submissive ones, women whom—according to Buck Clayton and others—she herself would sometimes treat to a dose of violence. Holiday told Memry Midgett that as a teenager in Baltimore, she would "play the part of a man" and put her girls out on the block, pimping them herself. If this kind of madness and pain was what made her singing so great, one historian recently said, it also was what cost her her dignity and, finally, her life. No woman should have to pay such a price even to make great art.

Of course, Billie Holiday's sad story—especially the juicy parts with plenty of sex and blood—has been eminently exploitable. Any reporting of the facts can seem lurid and exploitive, and whether we call her a natural or not, her life story has a natural salability. Here was the touching story of a pathetic victim, a crushed crazy lady. She *was* the blues. She *was* "strange fruit." Poor Miss Holiday!

According to another view of Holiday, she was a "sick person," the embodiment of our society's ills. Advertising this perspective on Holiday's life, the last sections of *Lady Sings the Blues* (the book) are threaded with confessions and lectures about her drug addiction/illness and its perils. Compellingly, she describes herself as someone who is not deserving of criminal action but of medical attention. Here the story taps another mythic line in which she was not only the hapless pawn in a game of cops and druggies but also the maimed modern antihero. Like Holden Caulfield of *Catcher in the Rye*—or, more to the point, Charlie Parker—she was sick; she was a scapegoat. Her illness was not just drug addiction but her predicament as a supremely sensitive person who lived in a crassly indifferent world. Our identification with her, according to this view, is mediated by our view of her as a sacrificial lamb sent to slaughter in order to appease strange new gods and to permit the rest of us to live on. This view may help explain some of the morbid appeal that she had during the final months of her life onstage, when at times she seemed to be disintegrated before our very eyes.

My own view is that Holiday's life was an audacious self-invention by a person who figured out very early that she was born into a situation of

Jan 12 1955

Dear Miss Bankhead:

I thought I was a friend of yours. That's why there was nothing in my book that was unfriendly to you, unkind or libelous. Because I didn't want to drag you I tried six times last month to talk to you on the damn phone, and tell you about the book just as a matter of courtesy. That bitch you have who impersonates you kept telling me to call back and when I did it was the same deal until I gave up.

But while I was working out of town, you didn't mind talking to Doubleday and suggesting behind my damn back that I had flipped and/or made up those little mentions of you in my book.

Baby, Cliff Allan and Billy Heywood are still around. My maid who was with me at the Strand isn't dead either. There are plenty of others around who remember how you carried on so you almost got me fired out of the place. And if you want to get shitty, we can make it a big shitty party. We can all get funky together.

I don't know whether you've got one of those damn lawyers telling you what to do or not. But I'm writing this to give you a chance to answer back quick and apologize to me and to Doubleday. Read my book over again. I understand they sent you a duplicate manu-script. There's nothing in it to hurt you. If you think so, let's talk about it like I wanted to last month. It's going to press right now so there is no time for monkeying around.

Straighten up and fly right, Banky. Nobody's trying to drag you.

Miss Tallulah Bankhead
Hotel Elysee
60 E. 54th St.

BILLIE HOLIDAY
% Dufty
43 West 93rd St
Apt. 17

comprehensive powerlessness. She was black, female, and poor. She was a "bastard" whose father was seldom around, whose mother was rejected by the rest of the family, and who was herself rejected. She was an outcast. The Cult of True Womanhood was pressed on her, with modifications tailored to her special situation as a black woman: if she were a good girl who worked hard, "good jobs" as a domestic servant and wife/mother were readily available to her. She could earn the right to show she was better than most representatives of her race and sex, better than her naughty mother.

Quite unconsciously at first, Eleanora Fagan began to destroy this conventional model of what her life had to be. She was a tomboy — pitcher on the sandlot hardball team, biker, skater, fistfighter. She refused to be Eleanora, Sadie's good girl; she was Bill or Billie, wild Clarence's hard daughter.

She would not attend school and chose friends who were like herself, "don't-carish." I believe that she began to hang out at East Baltimore's houses of prostitution both to hear good music and to observe close-up an alternative world where black women had some of the things she wanted: fancy clothes and jewelry, money of their own, and status beyond the realm of being a good little girl. This underworld cared nothing about conventional values and believed that the square world was there only to exploit. The nightlife women at Alice Dean's and Ethel Moore's were businesswomen as well as protected queens within a group that was decidedly aristocratic in its tastes and orientation toward life. Holiday was welcome in this fast world because she was pretty, clever, and tough. That she could sing was not just good for business; it also made her fun to have around and confirmed the group value of musical excellence. This was an aristocratic court that loved its "Empress of the Blues," Bessie Smith, as well as its other titled constituents.

In the dangerous substratum through which she moved, Holiday specifically chose tough men as boyfriend/pimps because she needed rock-hard partners. In exchange for her cash and sexual favors, she received greater freedom of movement and power. This was a fast and violent realm where alliances between night women and their men spelled not just exploitation but mutual dealing in a situation where power, for both pimp and prostitute, was the name of the game.

Singing gave her power. She had something rare, something prized within the group. From her own point of view, it gave her a ticket into the most private houses of the black night scene, and it gave her something more than even "self-esteem." It gave her art, a way of making sense of the crazy twenties, crazy Baltimore, and her crazy family and crazy life. It gave her a way of ordering

Holiday in Paris, 1954. (facing page)

experience, of placing her particular stamp on the past and even stylizing the present as it raced past her. All artists make a new world to live in. In that sense, they *are* godlike, as the Romantics claimed. As we have seen, Holiday's idea of what she had to do as a jazz singer was incredibly demanding. According to her aesthetic values, her job was not just to interpret songs but to be able to turn their tunes and the meaning of their lyrics "completely around." Here was a modernist on fire. Out of Tin Pan Alley dross or even Ellington gold, she cut her own new crown to wear. In the modernists' view, she did her ultimate job: she made it new. She had found a story of her own to tell in her own way; she had found a source of transcendent power.

One is reminded of Bernice Johnson Reagon's statement that during the civil rights movement of the 1960s, activists who were jailed often would raise a song of freedom within the spaces of their confinement. Their blended voices not only linked them together, but somehow the very lifting of the song itself seemed to change the balance of power within the jail. Sometimes, these activists report, those songs of life struck terror into the southern jailers' eyes. The music itself had an unfathomable power. That is the transformative power in art—what the poet Michael Harper called a "power beyond definition"—that Holiday discovered, and it is the mighty secret of her undying appeal.

•   •   •

May 25, 1959. Billie Holiday was booked by Leonard Feather to do a benefit concert at the Phoenix Theater in Greenwich Village. She had not been working much. Her body was a topographical map of needle marks and scar tissue. She was drinking a quart of gin every day, starting when she woke up. She had no appetite for food, but she still cared about her work. *Lady in Satin* had pleased her immensely. She was glad to get the fancy fiddles working behind *her;* it had seemed as if Ella Fitzgerald and Sarah Vaughan could get them anytime they wanted. Now, for once, *she* had been able to hear herself in this cushy musical setting. She would do this concert, she thought, then play Toronto and put together another record with strings.

She took a cab downtown and arrived early at the theater. She liked to get in early enough to rest and go through her routine of making up, which was harder than ever now that she made up not just her face but her arms and legs as well. Steve Allen, the comedian, was the emcee and arrived backstage at the Phoenix not long after Billie did. He recalled:

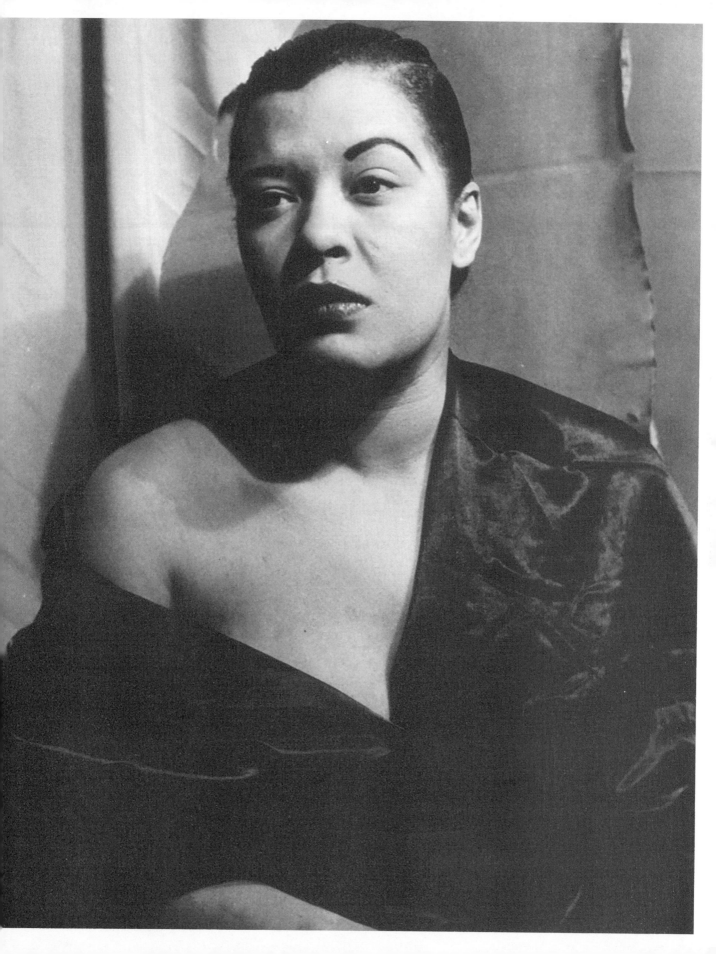

Holiday's passport, obtained for her European tour. Note that Holiday listed her place of birth as Philadelphia. To obtain the passport, her agent had to verify her birthplace by checking with the House of the Good Shepherd, where she had been detained as a ten-year-old.

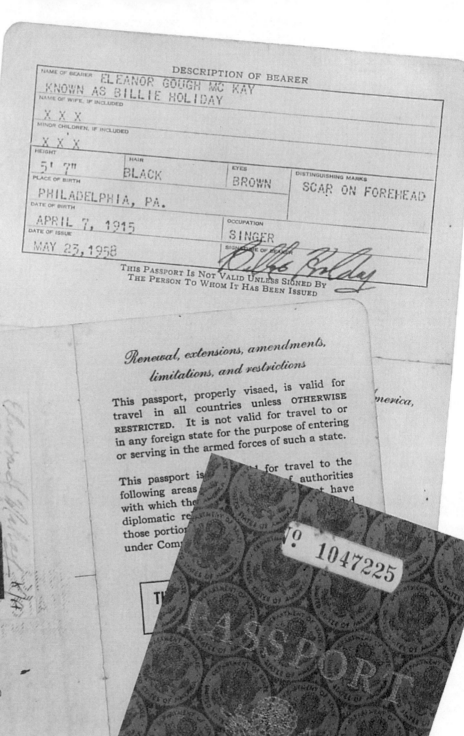

There might have been a musician on the stage putting his drums together, and there was somebody backstage like a stage manager or stagehand. And I asked, "Where do I go? I'm Steve Allen,. I'm on the show tonight." And he said, "Go anywhere." So I just walked into a room, and there was a little old Negro lady sitting on a cot or something in the corner. And just to be polite, I said, "Hello, how are you?" She said, "Fine, how's it going?" Something like that. I said, "Okay." And since I didn't know her, I walked to the other end of the room and just looked at my fingernails for a few minutes. And suddenly I had a very creepy feeling. And I did a very slow double-take, and the little old lady was Billie, looking forty years older than I expected to see her. The last time she had been fifty pounds heavier and a lovely looking person.... So suddenly seeing her skinny as a rail—looking like someone you see in pictures out of Dachau, looking very skinny, very skinny arms, very old. I don't know what kind of clothes she had on, but they were very poor, like a poor person would wear. It was very creepy. The lighting was very poor in the room, like maybe one single light bulb, very old theater. When the time came for her to perform, I introduced her as 'none other than the great Billie Holiday.' And somebody had to help her on the stage — It was Leonard Feather and me. We finally got her to the mike and we left her there and she sang terribly, of course, her voice was all scratchy, no vitality, no volume, nothing.

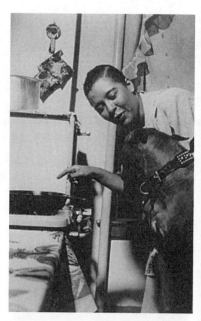

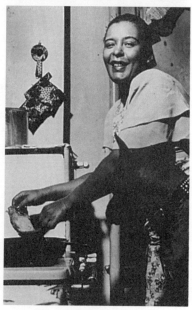

Leonard Feather, who had helped set up the show, also checked with Holiday backstage before the Phoenix appearance and was shook up to see her looking emaciated and obviously out of control. "I almost burst into tears when I saw her," he later told an interviewer. Holiday turned her face to his. "What's the matter, Leonard, you seen a ghost or something?" she asked. She looked hard at him.

Feather had seen her two months before at a party she had thrown to celebrate her forty-fourth birthday. She had looked somewhat better then, he remembered, but still Feather's memories of the party were mainly gloomy. "I think she had given up on life. I think the birthday party was given because she felt it would be the last birthday she would have." Friends came from all over the city. Along with Feather were the Duftys, George Wein, Jo Jones, Tony Scott and his wife, Ed Lewis, Annie Ross, and many others. She was living on Eighty-

Holiday at home on West 87th Street. Posing for the photographer, she pretends to let her dog know that supper is in the pan.

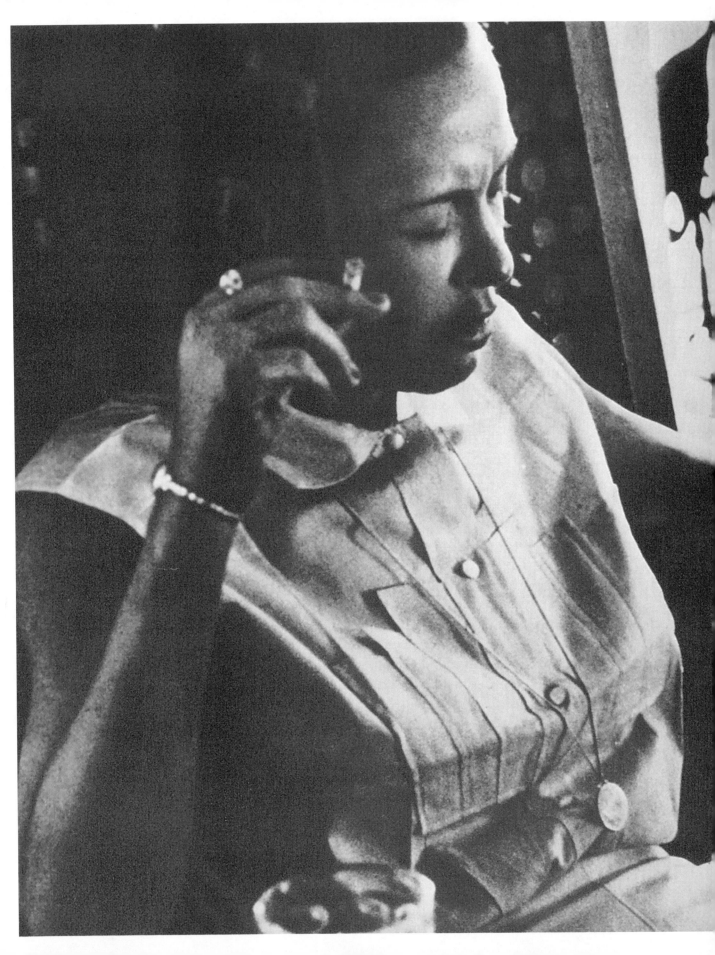

seventh Street, just off Columbus Avenue. Her place was on a pretty part of the street and consisted of what was euphemistically called a "garden apartment." It was one big room with a full kitchen off one end and a bedroom at the back. A large window overlooked a courtyard and garden. For the party she had put little tables of food in front of the window.

She had looked very weak and sick but still she had been enthusiastic. She had worn a stunning outfit and had cooked a meal —William Dufty called it a "hungry orphan's diet"— of fish stuffed with hamburger and peppers, with salad, chicken, greens, and black-eyed peas that brought back the old days when Sadie Fagan had been alive and would wait on all of Billie's friends. Feather had hinted then that she ought to check herself into a hospital and get some rest. She had told him that she was not going into a hospital; she did not trust them. (Some people who knew her said that she had a fear of hospitals because she could not easily get heroin there.) She would rather die at home. Anyway, she had no intention of dying. She had an idea for a new record, and she had gigs to do.

After the disturbing Phoenix show, Feather called Holiday's agent, Joe Glaser, and said that something had to be done for her. He also called Allen Morrison, an editor at *Ebony* whom he knew Holiday trusted. The three of them went to her apartment. Glaser did most of the talking. "She was lying down on the couch," Feather recalled, "and Glaser did everything he could to convince her that she had to go to the hospital right away and that she was in no condition to do any more work. No, she said that she had to open in Toronto next Monday and that she wasn't that sick and she would be all right. Maybe after an hour's conversation, nothing much seemed to be accomplished, and so we left."

She also brushed off others who advised her to check into a hospital. After all, she had cured herself before — usually with heroin or gin — and she had very good days along with the bad. Just a few months before, in October 1958, she and Mal Waldron had gotten together with Benny Carter, Buddy DeFranco, and Gerry Mulligan and done a set for the Monterey Jazz Festival that had won encore after encore. As the recording of that date shows, she was in fairly good voice, and the band was popping. Why give in and go to a hospital now? She had her own doctor. She had close friends helping her keep her life together. Alice Vrbsky, who was one of them, did most of the shopping for Lady and took her clothes to the cleaners. And they would watch television or listen to records together and just relax. The young singer Frankie Freedom also helped out, running errands for Holiday and keeping her company. One of his jobs probably was to buy her drugs and to keep the "works" clean and available.

This picture, taken at Holiday's home in the spring of 1959, is one of the last known photographs of the singer.

(facing page)

Holiday, 1958, at the recording session for *Lady in Satin*. Mal Waldron, the piano player on many of that record's tunes, said that this famous picture by Milt Hinton—and another showing her holding what appears to be a water glass full of something more potent than water— misrepresents the Holiday of this era and even this session. Despite her undeniable troubles, Waldron said, she was quite happy to be recording with old friends and with Ray Ellis's strings. "Take a picture fifteen seconds later," Waldron noted, "and you'd see her hugging one of her buddies and laughing like crazy."

(overleaf)

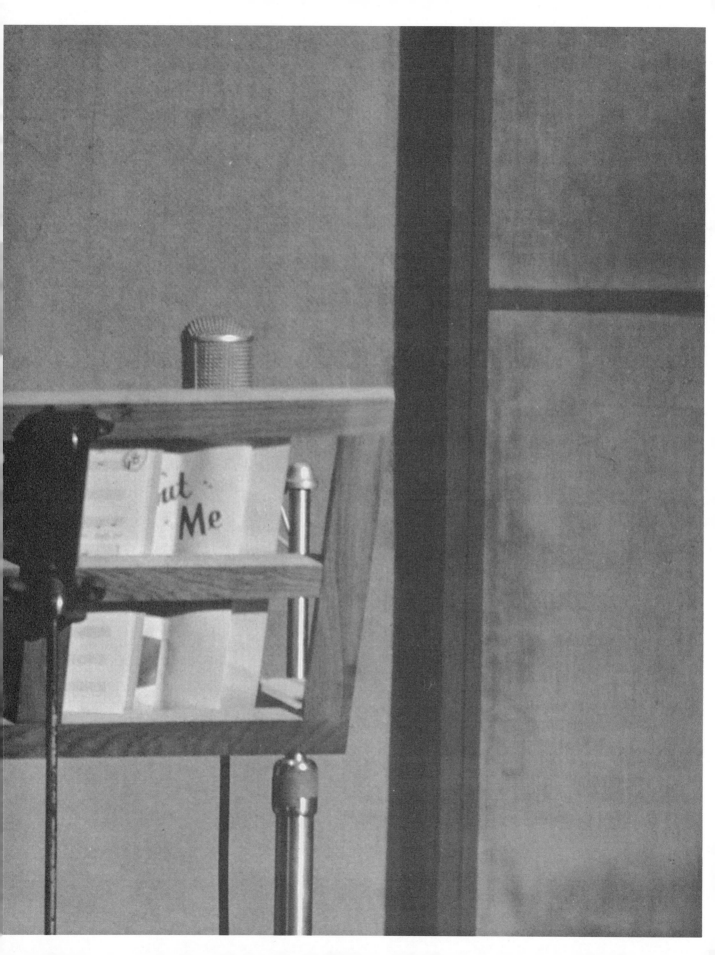

Louis McKay, c. 1953.

When Annie Ross was in town, she would stop by frequently. Sometimes she would do Lady's hair or give her a bath.

One night when Freedom came over to check on Holiday, he found her passed out on the floor. He knew he was not supposed to call the hospital—she had always told him not to—but when he picked her up to put her to bed, it was like picking up a corpse. He called an ambulance. He gave the address and said that Mrs. Eleanora McKay was extremely ill. Yes, it was an emergency.

The attendants in the emergency room at Knickerbocker Hospital took one look at the network of needle marks that scored her body and decided that she had had some sort of drug-related crisis. They had never heard of "Mrs. Eleanora McKay," of course, so she received no special treatment. She was just another poor, colored junkie woman. They put her on a cot, parked her in the hallway, and went about their business.

Finally, someone called her private doctor, Earl Caminer. He had her moved to Metropolitan Hospital—first to a ward and then, as her friends with money and pull began to take measure of the situation, to a private room. At first no one could get in to see her, as hospital policy permitted only family members to visit people in her condition. Kay Kelly, daughter of Phil Gough (Sadie's first legal husband), was not a blood relative, but she insisted she was Holiday's sister and was admitted. (Kelly knew that some of Holiday's close friends resented her, but she also knew that on more than one occasion, she had been the one to come up with the cash to bail Holiday out of trouble.) William Dufty showed his press pass and got in. Joe Glaser pulled an old trick and sent Louis McKay a plane ticket from California. He was still Holiday's legal husband, though they had long been estranged. Glaser felt that McKay, who had a little money of his own, could be used to run errands inside and outside the hospital. And maybe McKay could even help get Holiday sprung from the place.

Dufty had seen Holiday shortly before her hospitalization. On that night, he had picked up his phone and she had said only, "Can you come over?"

"Yes," he answered, and hung up. He started out the door, then went back to get his typewriter. He took a cab six blocks to her apartment and rushed to her door. Lady Day was there, looking very disturbed but glad that Dufty had come to help out. Another woman was there, presumably Elaine Swayne. Holiday introduced her as Lester "Prez" Young's girlfriend. Young had died two months before, and Holiday had taken it very hard. At his funeral, she had told several friends that she would be next. She had been glad to hear about this woman who

age Warns Va. School B...

CHICAGO, ILLINOIS—THURSDAY, JUNE 4, 1959

BILLIE HOLIDA...
SERIOUSLY ILL

(See...

Blue Note For Lady Day

BILLIE HOLIDAY, whose spectacular career has seesawed through the years to soaring heights and dismal depths, is critically ill in New York's Metropolitan hospital. The internationally famous blues singer, popularly known as "Lady Day," was rushed to the hospital after suffering an attack in her New York apartment. She's shown wrapped in mink and cuddling a Chihuahua during a recent appearance.

had taken care of Young. "Prez had a buffer. Someone to love him. Something I could never get," Holiday had told Dufty. But then at the funeral, Prez's legal spouse, Mary Young, had stepped in and taken full charge of everything, leaving the woman who had stayed with him at the end completely out of the picture. (On top of that, she had not permitted Holiday to sing at the funeral, which she wanted to do. Mary Young later said that Lady had looked so bad that she was afraid she would create a scene.) Now Holiday wanted Dufty to tell the real story of this woman "from a high class family" who had sacrificed everything for Young, comforting him and getting him whatever he needed. "It's a beautiful fucking love story," Holiday told Dufty. And she cried bitterly. *"It's a beautiful fucking love story."* Dufty did not want to write it, but it was not the time to argue. He left saying that he doubted the public would want to hear the story but that he would be willing to help get it organized.

The year was 1959, and William and Maely Dufty had just returned from a Memorial Day out of the city when someone from the *New York Post* called to tell him about a line in a gossip column casually announcing that Lady Day was in Metropolitan Hospital. His and Maely's first question, once they had found out she was still alive, was "How will she get drugs?" They feared she would die from the pain of withdrawal before anyone could get a chance to treat her other ailments.

In a 1973 interview, Dufty said he was "terrified," when he saw her for the first time in the hospital:

> *The thing I remember was that she had hollows here, in the temples. And it gives you an Oriental look, and that was scary. She was weak, but she was completely conscious. She was never one to waste words, anyway; the grip and the economy were still there…. And she said something that day about a comeback. "They'll call this a comeback." She didn't seem like someone who was dying. The oxygen tent was there, but she was not covered.*

Obviously, she was in good humor, and she said that she felt okay. As for drugs, at first she had brought stuff in with her. Eventually, she was put on methadone, so that while she was in the hospital, she was not bothered by withdrawal symptoms. What she needed were cigarettes. Nobody would bring her any. Dufty left her the ones he had and then changed to her brand, Pall Mall, and pretended to leave a pack by accident every day. She also needed some

Fearful of a scene, Lester Young's widow did not permit Holiday to sing at his funeral. Thus barred from paying a final tribute to her old collaborator and friend, Holiday broke down and cried miserably as she was taken outside by fellow musicians. Finally consoled at a nearby bar, her mood turned to anger at herself for losing control. "No matter what they do to you," she once told Hazel Scott, "never let 'em see you cry!"

bread, she said. He did not ask why. If she needed money, presumably for drugs, he would get it for her.

At once he began a series of pieces for the *Post* on Holiday's hospitalization. But that was his job and meant no extra cash, so he began to scout around to see which magazines might buy a special article about her sickbed drama. At first nobody was buying. *Playboy* said no. *Esquire* already had someone doing a piece. Then one day Dufty was in Holiday's room and noticed a stack of *Confidential* magazines, Holiday's favorite, on a table. Through an agent, Dufty offered *Confidential* the piece. An editor agreed, as long as it had a new angle and could be turned in before Holiday's death. They did not do obits.

Dufty already had a piece ready. For a new angle, he suggested the title "How Heroin Saved My Life." Framing it as an autobiographical confession piece, he rewrote what he had already done, this time in a *Confidential* tell-all voice. The magazine changed the title to "I Needed Heroin to Live" and

The TRUE Story of

BILLIE HO

See Series on Page 4

substantially rewrote the article to make it more fast paced and sentimental. But it paid right away, and Dufty gave Holiday the roughly $840 he had earned. She gave him $90 back for his trouble.

Meanwhile, Louis McKay had arrived from California. Between daily visits with Holiday, he busied himself with other projects. According to Holiday's former pianist, Carl Drinkard, McKay had originally been just one of many young fellows who had thought themselves in love with Holiday and liked to flirt with her. McKay had stood out because he was arrestingly handsome, boyishly romantic, fun to go to bed with, and a very tough guy. After a nightmare affair with John Levy, by all accounts the worst of them all (Levy was an exceptionally violent man, who took all her money and then, when he had used her up, arranged to have her arrested for possessing dope that was actually his), young McKay had not looked too bad. But their affair was stormy and very violent. As Drinkard told it, Holiday eventually came to feel trapped by both men. The pattern she

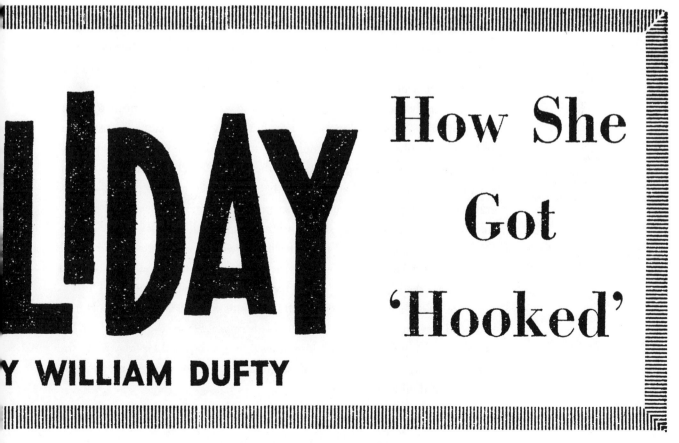

June 16, 1959

Seeks Police Removal From Billie's Side

NEW YORK — (UPI) — Blues singer Billie Holiday's lawyer took steps Monday to remove a police guard from outside her hospital room.

The room was placed under guard Friday after Miss Holiday was booked by telephone on charges of possessing narcotics. Police charged that she had a quanity of heroin with her in Metropolitan hospital, where she is being treated for a disease of the liver and a heart ailment.

Earle W. Zaidine, the 43-year-old singer's attorney, appeared at Police Headquarters Monday with a writ of habeas corpus. A hearing is set for Tuesday in Manhattan Supreme Court.

Miss Holiday was admitted to the hospital May 31.

Holiday, June 1959. To the end, the media described Holiday as a "blues singer," much to her consternation, and seemed to delight in reporting her woes. Why else print a file photo of her looking like a clown? What is not emphasized in this article is that one of the country's greatest singers had been arrested in her hospital bed.

(above and facing page)

had always known—of love affair as deal or as mutual exploitation—had fallen apart under Levy's iron rule because, as a famous junkie who could not score on her own, she had been desperately dependent on Levy every day. And every day brought a new drama concerning whether she would get her fix on time and what she would have to do to get it. Eventually McKay brought more of the same.

Specialist in power quests that she was, she would try to throw the machinery of entrapment into reverse. For example, she would insist that Levy or McKay pick fights with guys she claimed had insulted her, then stand back and watch them do battle, sometimes for their lives. "Everything would be going fine," Drinkard said, "then Lady would start something." Like many abused women who cannot seem to think for themselves anymore and whose every decision is based on what they think their master-men want, Holiday would strike out. She would pick fights with Levy or McKay, and even if she was badly defeated (often she could not go onstage because she had received too obvious a beating), she could have the satisfaction of seeing the controller of her life thrown, by her unexpected machinations, suddenly out of control. She would intentionally mention taboo subjects, such as the money she earned and where it went, or she would call them taboo names (McKay hated it when she called him a "motherfucker"), and then all hell would break loose. If one of those fights broke out in public, Drinkard said, McKay would drag her into another room, turn his ring around, and hit her hard enough to knock her out cold. Then he would let her sleep it off.

No doubt Holiday felt that although she was a singer/prostitute to these manager/pimps—not walking the streets but performing in clubs or onstage six and seven nights a week—she would at least remind them occasionally that she was not being fooled by their swagger or their tricks. Surely she knew for herself what Carl Drinkard says that he knew: that McKay had married not for love or even just for money, but because as his wife she could not testify against him in court if he got caught dealing drugs or otherwise breaking the law.

Holiday must have had mixed feelings when she saw McKay at her door in Metropolitan Hospital. He was not there long before he showed her a contract turning over the rights to *Lady Sings the Blues* to him. He also needed Dufty's signature. Dufty would not sign but did not want to anger McKay so much that he would leave town and ruin her chances for release from the hospital. So he played along, saying he was thinking it over, and he advised Holiday to do the same. She liked the idea of the deal, she told McKay, but thought they should hold out for double the money.

In brighter spirits as the days passed, she talked with Dufty and all her visitors about doing a new record. Someone said that she looked so good that maybe she should make a record from her hospital room: "Call it 'Lady at the Met'!" She loved the idea and began to announce it as her new project.

And then bad luck again befell her. A nurse found a tinfoil packet of heroin in her room and reported that she had seen dots of the white stuff around Holiday's nose. The singer vehemently denied that the heroin was hers or that she had been sniffing it. Dufty and others said that she was not using heroin anymore and that someone must have left the stuff there as a misguided favor or a malicious plant. She was too weak to sit up, much less walk across the room to sniff dope, Maely Dufty said. In spite of these efforts, Holiday was arrested in her hospital bed. She could not be moved, so a guard was stationed outside her door. The police even arranged to have her radio and record player taken away and to curtail all special extras: no more comic books or *Confidential* magazines. In daily front-page articles in the *New York Post,* Dufty called for the mayor or someone in power to protect Lady Day from this final indignity, all to no avail.

Only a few people contacted Holiday at the hospital—the Duftys, Leonard Feather, Alice Vrbsky, Detroit Red, Louis McKay, "Sister" Kay Kelly, Joe Glaser, Francis Church (Glaser's assistant), lawyers, and a few others. To scare up more callers, Dufty ran a piece in the *Post* announcing that cards were flowing in and the room was full of flowers. He even named names of friends from whom she had not heard, trying to shame them into action. The trick worked, and a few more people called or sent flowers.

Though now in an oxygen tent all the time, "she was brave," Nat Hentoff (relying on Dufty) reported. "At the slightest rattle of the oxygen tent she lunged forward, dukes up, and barked out sharp orders, commanding those about her to slow down to her tempo; 'Don't be in such a hurry!'" Gradually, Lady sank into what the hospital called a coma. "She was not unconscious," Dufty recalled. "That was the official version of reality. She was just semi-comatose and resting; and she would maybe go into a period and come back and so it was like she was handling her energy…. They had her sort of propped up…. She was breathing with great difficulty…. she was squeezing my hand. As long as she wasn't fighting the pain, her face was beautiful. She had gained weight. She looked beautiful."

She had been hospitalized for forty-four days when a chaplain came to administer the last rites of the Roman Catholic Church. One hour before her death, a nurse came to Dufty, who was in the hallway, and said that while attending to Holiday, she had found the $750 from the *Confidential* piece and

PAGE 2

Arrest III 'Lady Day', On Dope Rap

NEW YORK — (UPI) — Blues singer Billie Holiday, critically ill with liver a n d heart ailments, was arrested Friday for allegedly sniffing heroin in her hospital bed.

The famed "Lady Day" 43, was booked by telephone after a nurse told police she seized a package of white powder—later shown to be heroin—from Miss Holiday.

The nurse had become suspicious when she saw some of the white powder on Miss Holiday's face.

Police said Miss Holiday admitted she occasionally took heroin. She told authorities she found the heroin in the bottom of her pocketbook after she was admitted to Metropolitan hospital May 31.

However, police believed a visitor had smuggled the heroin to her. They said they would question all her previous visitors.

When she entered the hospital last month, her attorney said Miss Holiday had "whipped" her narcotics addiction.

Police said she would be arraigned at bedside when she is well enough.

BILLIE HOLIDAY

that the singer had said she wanted someone named Bill to have it. "Are you Bill?" the nurse asked. Holiday had twisted the money into a cigarette-like roll, taped it tight, and hidden it well. The nurse found it, not taped to her leg as Dufty decided to say in the press at the time, but up her vagina. ("She knew where to hide things," Dufty later said.) To the nurse he replied, "You take it to the office as part of her property." For the first time, Dufty felt that she was going to die, that she knew it, and that there was nothing to be done.

She was asleep, but she seemed to rally, Dufty said. She was looking strong but breathing very deeply, struggling for air. Two nurses were in attendance. One of them told Dufty that as long as she was breathing, she was fighting for life. He could see the fight in her face as she gasped for breath. She looked beautiful. Then her face relaxed. The nurse felt her pulse. "She's gone," she said. The official report was that she had had serious heart, kidney, and liver ailments that were fatally complicated by a lung blockage.

Holiday's funeral, July 21, 1959, at St. Paul the Apostle Church, New York. (preceding overleaf)

Those at Holiday's grave site included, from left, William Dufty, Maely Dufty, and Joe Glaser among others including Little Jimmy Scott.

Dufty's first idea for the funeral was St. Patrick's Cathedral, but it could not be arranged. So the ceremony was held at St. Paul the Apostle Cathedral on Sixtieth Street at Ninth Avenue. Unlike many funerals of jazz figures, Holiday's involved no departures from the formal Catholic Requiem High Mass, with the full cathedral choir providing the music. There had been a wake the day before, with Lady Day dressed in her favorite pink lace stage gown and gloves.

Three thousand people attended the funeral service. Five hundred others stood outside. When it was over, the musicians who knew her well did not gather as usual at a nearby watering hole to give a New Orleans–style toast and celebrate the life of the newly dead. They just stood around on the street outside the church. There was a great silence broken only by the shuffling of feet. Then everyone went home.

·   ·   ·

Associated Booking Corp.

JOSEPH G. GLASER, PRESIDENT

745 FIFTH AVENUE
NEW YORK 22, N. Y.
Phone PLAZA 9—4600

203 NORTH WABASH AVE.
CHICAGO, ILL.
Phone CENTRAL 6—9451

407 LINCOLN ROAD
MIAMI BEACH, FLA.
Phone JEFFERSON 8—0383

8619 SUNSET BOULEVARD
HOLLYWOOD 46, CALIF.
Phone OLYMPIA 2—9940

FROM NEW YORK OFFICE

CABLE ADDRESS: STARBOOK, NEW YORK

August 18-1959

Mr. William Dufty,
43 W. 93rd St.,
New York City.

Dear Bill —

I just returned to the office, having been ill periodically for the past two weeks, and was amazed when Frances Church advised me that Mele had been in an automobile accident and was in the Flower Hospital. I sincerely hope it is nothing serious and that she will be back feeling her usual self very shortly.

I greatly appreciate your sending me the correspondance with Barry Shear, and am writing him that I will be in California in the next few days, and available to see him at his convenience, however, it is a pleasure to advise you that I have personally been talking to Otto Preminger whom I have known for many years, with regard to doing Billie's story with the understanding he would work from your book, and in my conversation with Otto, he was thrilled to learn that we now exclusively represent Dorothy Dandridge who would be most happy to portray Billie, which I believe you would agree should really be something, especially with Otto Preminger doing it. however, Billy, I am not disregarding exploring other possibilities, and hope to have word for you when I return from the West Coast.

Frances will be in touch with Mele and if you want to get a message to me, I can be reached in care of my California Office, or Frances will convey anything you wish.

With every good wish to Mele and yourself,

As ever,

JOE GLASER.

jg—c

Two things stand out in these final scenes of Billie Holiday's life. The first is that even at the last, people were bargaining with her over her story and how it would be told. Quite typically, she gave Dufty permission to write anything he saw fit in order to raise money. And quite typically, the story was a sensationalized one, substantially true but aimed at a popular audience caring more to have myths confirmed than truths confronted. Although she seemingly avoided giving Louis McKay the movie rights to her autobiography, he got them anyhow. She died leaving no will (her lawyer had kept after her to do one, but she thought wills were bad luck), and so McKay inherited her estate and lived out the rest of his life on her royalties and permissions fees. His sons, no relation to Holiday, now collect this money.

Biographer Phyllis Rose has said that women are often fiercely protective of their life stories. Sometimes, Rose says, their stories are virtually all they have, and even if they have manufactured them (perhaps *especially* if they have manufactured them), they try hard to permit no one to tell their tales except themselves.

Surely Billie Holiday's was an invented life, pieced together from myths and dream/wishes as well as memories. And yet surely, too, she was willing to trade her life story, again and again, for cash on the spot. Often she seemed not to care what story was told in her name as long as she was paid. How does her evidently carefree attitude toward her story fit with Rose's compelling thesis?

I think the answer lies in another fascinating aspect of her final days. Until the end, she was planning to make that next gig, cut that next record. "Lady at the Met" was the joke that stood for her intention to keep producing as an artist. Her true story was not in the throwaway articles or books, even if they pretended to have been written by her. My guess is that despite the triteness and utter falseness of the Hollywood movie *Lady Sings the Blues,* she would have enjoyed it. It was a touching tale that brought her publicity and raised cash.

But the story she *would* fight over was in her music. That was "all she had," all that really mattered—the precious thing that was, as Ralph Ellison said of the slaves and their music, what she had in place of freedom. As a very young singer, she had developed a gift for looking at a song's lyrics, listening (with the help of someone who read music) to its melody, and then transforming both until they were hers. She recomposed them to such a degree that she was not just an actress who played a part; she was an artist who created roles that included criticisms of the roles as written as well as something of her own, her own story.

What stories did her music tell? Sometimes she told tales of romance, she made the most yearning of love tales complex and earnest enough to be believable.

A month after Holiday's death, Joe Glaser worked on a way to get her story on film. Described here is one of the many movie ideas that were scrapped. *Lady Sings the Blues* (1972), with Diana Ross as Holiday, has been the only Hollywood feature film purporting to tell Holiday's history. (facing page)

Sometimes she told tales of love on the rocks, and she could be cool and silvery or smolder with anger. Almost always her stories were told in a spare musical vocabulary. Whether she used elements of parody, farce, or tragedy, she told her stories in the most understated way and with a few concentrated notes that seemed to signify a million notes restrained.

She was a blues heroine because whatever the written lyrics of her songs, even when they were self-pitying, her voice was always, *always,* the heroine of the story in her music. With her elegance, unfailing swing, hornlike timbre, and brilliant impulse for reinvention, she blew the blues away.

She turned her masklike faces against the blue-devil blues and scattered them to the four winds. She made up her mind; she made up her face. She wore the masks not only to conceal and to protect her secret self but also in the tradition of the African ritual mask, which, as André Malraux has observed, can offer talismanic protections against entropy, against the mood called the blues. Bernice Johnson Reagon reminds us, too, that in many African societies, the mask worn in a ritual setting is a created face, a stylized face that is "omnipresent, all-powerful, beyond human boundaries." It is worn, she says, by "one with human frailties who offers herself to the powers of the gods so that her voice can find the air." Thus, the mask is both a protection and a medium.

Never far in spirit from the good-time houses where she started out, Holiday partied hard with her voice. "I ain't got no legit voice," she told a group of musicians she was rehearsing. What she had instead was the greatest jazz voice of the century. And in the end, she received the power she had angled for throughout her short, often unhappy life. The much-exploited story of her life in Baltimore and New York and on the road has a certain poignancy and lasting interest. But the story line in her recorded music — that mask, as it were — has transcendent power and will last as long as people care about the sad, beautiful truths of life and the hard-earned art to tell them.

Selected Bibliography

· · ·

Albertson, Chris. *Bessie*. New York: Stein & Day, 1972.

Balliett, Whitney. *Dinosaurs in the Morning: Forty-One Pieces on Jazz*. New York: Lippincott, 1962.

——. *Ecstasy at the Onion: Thirty-One Pieces on Jazz*. New York: Bobbs-Merrill, 1971.

——. "Night Clubs" (Profiles of Max Gordon and Barney Josephson). *The New Yorker*, October 9, 1971.

——. *Such Sweet Thunder*. New York: Bobbs-Merrill, 1966.

Baraka, Amiri. *Black Music*. New York: William Morrow & Co., 1968.

Bigard, Barney. *With Louis and the Duke: The Autobiography of a Jazz Clarinetist*. Edited by Barry Martyn. New York: Oxford, 1986.

Brooks, Michael. Booklets enclosed with the CD set *The Quintessential Billie Holiday*. Vols.# 1-8. CBS (1990-91).

Buchmann-Moller, Frank. *You Just Fight for Your Life: The Story of Lester Young*. New York: Praeger, 1990.

Carby, Hazel V. *Reconstructing Womanhood: The Emergence of the Afro-American Woman Novelist*. New York: Oxford, 1987.

Carter, Benny. Liner notes for *Sam Cooke: Tribute to the Lady*. Keen LP A2004 (c.1963).

Chilton, John. *Billie's Blues: The Billie Holiday Story, 1933-1959*. London: Quartet, 1975.

——. *Who's Who of Jazz*. New York: Time-Life, 1978.

Clayton, Buck. *Buck Clayton's Jazz World*. London: Macmillan, 1986.

Condon, Eddie. *We Called It Music*. New York: Henry Holt, 1947.

Coulter, Glenn. "Billie Holiday." In *The Art of Jazz: Essays in the Nature and Development of Jazz*. Edited by Martin Williams. New York: Oxford, 1959.

Crouch, Stanley. Liner notes for Billie Holiday LP "All or Nothing at All" Verve LP 2610-053 (1978).

Dance, Stanley. *The World of Count Basie*. New York: Scribner's, 1980.

——. *The World of Swing*. New York: Scribner's, 1974.

——. Liner notes for *Teddy Wilson and His All-Stars*. Columbia LP KG 31617 (1973).

Davis, Francis. *Outcats: Jazz Composers, Instrumentalists, and Singers*. New York: Oxford, 1990.

DeVeaux, Alexis. *Don't Explain: A Song of Billie Holiday*. New York: Harper & Row, 1980.

Down Beat, 1936 to 1991.

Ellison, Ralph. *Shadow and Act*. New York: Random House, 1964.

——. *Going to the Territory*. New York: Random House, 1986.

Feather, Leonard. *The New Edition of the Encyclopedia of Jazz*. New York: Horizon, 1960.

——. "Billie Holiday: A Love Revisited." Booklet enclosed with the LP set *Billie Holiday: "The Golden Years." Vol. 2*. Columbia C3L 40 (c. 1970).

——. Liner notes for "Billie Holiday: Strange Fruit." Atlantic SD 1614-0598 (1972).

——. *From Satchmo to Miles*. New York: De Capo, 1984.

Finkelstein, Sidney. *Jazz: A People's Music*. New York: Citadel, 1948.

Floyd, Samuel, ed. *Black Music in the Harlem Renaissance*. New York: Greenwood, 1990.

Giddins, Gary. *Rhythm-a-Ning: Jazz Tradition and Innovation in the 80s*. New York: Oxford, 1985.

Gleason, Ralph J. *Celebrating the Duke & Louis, Bessie, Billie, Bird, Carmen, Miles, Dizzy, and Other Heroes*. New York: Little, Brown, 1975.

Gourse, Leslie. *Louis' Children: American Jazz Singers*. New York: Quill, 1984.

Hammond, John, with Irving Townsend. *John Hammond on Record: An Autobiography*. New York: Summit, 1977.

Hardwick, Elizabeth. "Billie Holiday." *New York Review of Books*. 4 April, 1976.

Harper, Michael. Liner notes for *John Coltrane*. Prestige LP PR 24003 (c. 1972).

Harriott, Frank. *PM*. September 2, 1945.

Harrison, Daphne Duval. *Black Pearls; Blues Queens of the 1920s*. New Brunswick, N.J.: Rutgers, 1988.

Hentoff, Nat. "Billie Holiday: Ain't Nobody's Business If I Do." Booklet enclosed with the LP set *Billie Holiday: Ain't Nobody's Business If I Do*. Book-of-the-Month Records 90-5652.

———. *Jazz Is.* New York: Ridge, 1976.

———. "The Real Lady Day." *New York Times Magazine,* December 24, 1972.

Hoefer, George. "The Sound of Harlem." Booklet enclosed with the LP set *The Sound of Harlem.* Columbia C3L 33 (1962).

Holiday, Billie, with William Dufty. *Lady Sings the Blues.* New York: Doubleday, 1965.

James, Burnett . *Billie Holiday.* New York: Hippocrene, 1984.

Kaminsky, Max. *My Life in Jazz.* New York: Harper & Row, 1963.

Kernfeld, Barry. *The New Grove Encyclopedia of Jazz.* New York: Macmillan, 1988.

Kliment, Bud. *Billie Holiday, Singer.* New York: Chelsea House, 1990.

Kouwenhoven, John A.. *The Beer Can by the Highway.* New York: Doubleday, 1961.

Lewis, David Levering. *When Harlem Was in Vogue.* New York: Knopf, 1981.

Lyttelton, Humphrey. *The Best of Jazz. Vol. 2: Enter the Giants, 1931-1944.* New York: Taplinger, 1983.

Malraux, André. *Picasso's Mask.* New York: Holt, Rinehart & Winston, 1976.

Melody Maker, 1933 to 1959.

Mezzrow, Milton "Mezz," and Bernard Wolfe. *Really the Blues.* New York: Random House, 1946.

Morgenstern, Dan. "The Commodore Story: An Interview with Milt Gabler." Booklet enclosed with the LP set T*he Complete Commodore Jazz Recordings Vol. 1.* Mosaic Records 22-123 (1987).

Murray, Albert. *Good Morning Blues: The Autobiography of Count Basie.* New York: Random House, 1985.

———. *Stomping the Blues.* New York: McGraw-Hill, 1976.

Reed, Joseph W.. *Three American Originals: John Ford, William Faulkner, and Charles Ives.* Middletown, Conn.: Wesleyan, 1984.

Rose, Al. *Eubie Blake.* New York: Schimer, 1979.

Rose, Phyllis. *Jazz Cleopatra: Josephine Baker in Her Time.* New York: Doubleday, 1989.

Schuller, Gunther. *The Swing Era: The Development of Jazz, 1930-1945.* New York: Oxford, 1989.

Shapiro, Nat, and Nat Hentoff. *Hear Me Talkin' to Ya: The Story of Jazz by the Men Who Made It.* New York: Rinehart, 1955.

Shaw, Arnold. *The Street That Never Slept: New York's Fabled 52nd Street.* New York: DaCapo, 1971.

Shaw, Artie. *The Trouble with Cinderella: An Outline of Identity.* New York: Farrar, Straus & Young, 1952.

Smith, Charles Edward. "The Street." Booklet enclosed with the LP set *Swing Street.* Epic SN 6042 (1962).

Stewart, Rex. *Jazz Masters of the Thirties.* New York: Macmillan, 1972.

Taylor, Arthur. *Notes and Tones.* Liège, Belgium: Arthur Taylor, 1977.

Ulanov, Barry. *A Handbook of Jazz.* London: Hutchinson, 1958.

———. "What is Jazz?" In *Culture and the Arts,* edited by James Hall and Barry Ulanov. New York: McGraw-Hill, 1967.

White, John. *Billie Holiday.* New York: Universe Books, 1987.

Williams, Martin. *Where's the Melody? A Listener's Introduction to Jazz.* New York: Pantheon, 1966.

———. "Actress without an Act." *Jazz Journal,* October 1968,

———. "The Smithsonian Collection of Classic Jazz." Booklet enclosed with the CD set *The Smithsonian Collection of Classic Jazz.,* rev. ed. (1987).

Yamato, Akira. "Billie Holiday on Verve." Booklet enclosed with the LP set *Billie Holiday on Verve: 1946-1959.* Verve OOMJ 3480/9 (1985).

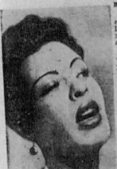

Remember Billie Holiday?

By JACK O'GRADY

St. Raymond's Catholic Cemetery at E. 177th St. and Lafayette Av. in the Bronx is nestled behind an office building and difficult to find.

And if you're going there to visit Billie Holiday's grave, you're in trouble, too.

It's No. 59, but the sad truth is that the numbers have disappeared.

Sadder too is the fact that no headstone marks the plot where Billie Holiday is buried.

Doesn't anyone care? Not even the managers and musicians, the record companies and sheet music houses that profited from her in life?

"Everybody I talked to," said George Crater, jazz commentator for WNCN-FM and columnist for Downbeat magazine.

"copped out with one excuse or another."

So Downbeat established the "Billie Holiday Marker Fund."

"A lot of people threw around telephone numbers," Crater said, "telling me they would have donated $1,000 or so for a tombstone, except for one reason or another. Ironically, under cemetery restrictions the most elaborate marker in the size permitted would only cost $300."

Crater became interested two weeks ago when, in reading Doris Lilly's column in The Post, he saw this:

"I drove out to The Bronx to take a look at Billie Holiday's grave, but it's a little hard to find as there is no stone or marking of any kind. Just No. 59."

"One guy who was indebted to Billie told me he thought a stone was ord——," Crater said.

"Then h claimed he was waiting for warm weather. Imagine, and Billie was buried last July.

"His last cop-out was that he thought it would be against his religion.

"Another excuse I got was that they were waiting for the ground to settle. All he had to do was check to learn there's a cement foundation behind the grave on which to place a marker."

Crater's appeal is being aided by Mrs. Elaine Lorillard, originator of the Newport Jazz Festival, jazz authority Leonard Feather, and Alan Morrison of Ebony magazine.

Billie Holiday will get her marker—if not from the money she earned for others, from the nickels, dimes, quarters and dollars of the millions of fans to whom she gave so much pleasure.

INSIDE THE POST

Amusements	16-23
Barry, Joseph	M9
Books	M11
Crossword Puzzle	M15
Editorials	M8
Franzblau, Dr. Rose N.	M10
Herblock	M9
Lyons, Leonard	M7
McGrory, Mary	M10
Movie Clock	20
Pogo	M6
Pet's	39
Radio	23
Roosevelt, Eleanor	M7
Sann, Paul	M6
Schools	24, 25
Shannon, William V.	M9
Skolsky, Sidney	M3
TV Programs	M12, 13
Watts, Richard	16
Williams, Bob	M13
Wilson, Earl	M3

Photo Credits

· · ·

Page *8*: **Robin Carson,** Courtesy of Avalon Archives

Page *11r., 12b., 34t.l., 34b., 34t.mid., 35b. 35t. 95l.*: **Alain Chevrier,** Courtesy of Francis Paudras

Page *36, 46r., 47l.*: **Maurey Garber Studio,** Courtesy of Avalon Archives

Page *79*: **Fred Hess & Son,** Courtesy of Avalon Archives

Page *182-183*: **Milt Hinton**

Page *4, 22, 49, 54, 90, 98, 130 164b., 164, 164t., 166, 179t., 179b., 186*: **Herman Leonard,** Courtesy of Francis Paudras

Page *37*: **Bill Mark,** Courtesy of Avalon Archives

Page *39, 42, 43, 143m., 143b., 143t.*: **Daniel Nilva**

Page *44*: **Robert Parent**

Page *53, 106b., 108, 109, 110, 111, 132b., 132m., 132t.*: **Charles Peterson**

Page *104, 122r., 122l., 123r., 123l.*: **Timme Rosenkrantz,** Courtesy of Avalon Archives

Page *26, 28, 29 32*: **Aaron Siskind**

Page *12m., 93, 171, 177*: **Carl Van Vechten**

Page *2, 10r., 10l., 11l., 125., 14l., 14r., 15r., 15l., 16-17, 19, 30, 31, 40, 41, 46l., 47r., 55, 58, 61, 62-63, 64, 65, 66, 68t., 68b., 69, 70-71, 72, 80, 92, 94r., 94l., 96, 102, 103, 105, 107, 114, 115, 118-119, 120, 126t., 126b., 127t., 127b., 129, 137t., 137b., 138, 139, 140, 141, 144, 145, 145b., 146b., 146t., 147, 148, 149, 150-151, 152b., 152t., 153, 154b., 154m., 154t., 155, 156, 157t., 157b., 158, 162, 163, 168r., 168l., 169, 170, 172, 173, 184, 185, 190, 191, 192-193, 195, 197*: Courtesy of Avalon Archives

Page *25, 57, 60, 73, 106t., 165*: Courtesy of Frank Driggs Collection

Page *161t., 161b., 178, 187, 188-189, 196, 145t.*: Courtesy of the Estate of Billie Holiday

Page *20*: Courtesy of Robert O'Meally

Page *6, 33, 160, 174, 180*: Courtesy of Francis Paudras

Page *76, 77, 84, 85*: Courtesy of Peale Museum, Baltimore

Page *50, 51, 86, 89, 95r., 113, 116, 124, 134-135, 199*: Courtesy of Ken Whitten Collection

After considerable ado and delay, a simple marker finally was placed on Holiday's grave in the Bronx. Her records are her true monuments; they will be around when the stones have crumbled. *(facing page)*

Discographical Notes

. . .

The most reliable discography of Billie Holiday's music is Akira Yamato's, which appeared in 1985 as a section of his booklet accompanying the ten-LP set *Billie Holiday on Verve, 1946-1959*. "Completist" Holidayites will be well served by the Yamato list (now available only from out-of-print record dealers or on loan from special libraries), and they should know that Yamato has promised an updated discography soon.

Recommending a selection of Billie Holiday albums or CDs is a special problem. She did not make whole albums of music in the sense that Duke Ellington or Frank Sinatra did, with all the pieces consciously assembled in support of thematic or formal principles of unity. As a recording artist, her form was not the whole album but the song—the two-and-a-half- to three-minute "cut," tailor-made, even late in her career, for the jukebox or radio market—or the concert of songs. Some of her most memorable records of the fifties were not originally set up as record dates as such but as concerts; in a real sense, her art form was the club set or the concert.

Her albums and CDs, then, all consist of compilations of songs from studio or "live" concert dates, sometimes both. They may be classified either as "complete works" (sometimes including outtakes, sometimes not), "greatest hits" of various kinds (spotlighting particular periods, labels, or genres, such as blues or torch songs), recorded concerts, or collections of studio work gathered under broad titles such as *Songs for Distingué Lovers* or *Velvet Mood*.

FIRST PERIOD (1933–1938)

For this period, completist collectors will want either the American or the Japanese compilations of Holiday's "complete works" on Columbia. The American set, titled *The Quintessential Billie Holiday,* so far consists of eight CDs or LPs. (The ninth and final one is due out in late 1991.) The Japanese box, consisting of ten CDs, is now complete and includes all available outtakes. For her recordings with Teddy Wilson, which are quite interesting to listen to in the context of Wilson's work with other vocalists or with no vocalist at all, I recommend the multivolume *Chronological Classics: Teddy Wilson and His Orchestra* (Classic Records, Paris, France.) This comprehensive collection is this era's only reasonably good Wilson recording available now that the superb LP *Teddy Wilson and His All-Stars* is out of print. By far the best collection of Holiday's greatest hits of this period is the extraordinary *Lady Day: A Collection of Classic Jazz Interpretations by Billie Holiday with All-Star Accompaniments*, a Columbia LP now available on a Japanese CD that includes four additional tracks.

For those wanting a disc or two of this outstanding material (and lacking the chance to secure either out-of-print or Japanese recordings), I recommend Columbia's *The Quintessential Billie Holiday,* volumes 2 and 4.

SECOND PERIOD (1939–1949)

As this book indicates, the second Holiday period was distinguished not by a shift in label—she stayed with Columbia Records until 1942—but by a shift in style. For the first part of this second period, turn to the later volumes in the complete works mentioned above. It is imperative to acquire all of Holiday's Commodore recordings, also done during this period. Mosaic Records has issued them as LPs, second takes and all, as part of the set called *The Complete Commodore Jazz Recordings*. Apart from the rest of the catalog, the Billie Holiday Commodores (minus the second takes) are available on CD from Commodore Records and, with far better audio fidelity, on a Japanese LP.

From this period come the first commercially available recordings of Holiday in concert. A fine collection of these "live" sessions is *Billie Holiday, Masters of Jazz*, volume 3. Verve's recordings of concerts at the Philharmonic, 1946, and at Carnegie Hall, 1947, have been issued as part of the "complete" LP box titled *Billie Holiday on Verve, 1946-1959*. Selections from these concerts also appear on the Verve CD *Compact Jazz Live*.

MCA/GRP's box containing the label's complete Holiday catalog, including second takes and songs never released before, is expected on the market by the fall, 1991. Meanwhile, I recommend the two-volume CD set *Lady's Decca Days*. Along with the Commodores, it is an excellent set from this period.

THIRD PERIOD (1950–1959)

The Verves headline this period, and, again, there is a box of ten LPs that includes everything. The good news is that a ten-CD set from Polygram, which owns the Verve masters, is due out any day. Those who cannot wait should know that none of Polygram/Verve's "greatest hit" collections on CD has done justice to the material, so look for the CD remakes of the original albums, which give you a sense of the original song sequences and cover art. In this category, I'd go for the three American reissues currently available on Polygram/Verve: *Songs for Distingué Lovers*, *Lady Sings the Blues*, and *The Essential Billie Holiday: Carnegie Hall Concert*. I am also watching for CD reissues of *All or Nothing at All* (now available on LP), *Solitude* (now on the two-LP set *First Verve Sessions*), and *Ella Fitzgerald and Billie Holiday: The Newport Years*.

For an excellent recording of Holiday "live" in Germany in 1954, pick up Blue Note's CD *Billie's Blues*. I also highly recommend *Lady in Satin* (on Columbia), Holiday's penultimate studio recording.

MISCELLANEOUS

Collectors will enjoy the four boxes (three CDs each) *Billie Holyday* [sic] *Live and Private Recordings in Chronological Order* (New Sound Planet). Here one finds Holiday's only recording with Duke Ellington, the sound track of the "Big City Blues (The Saddest Tale)" section of the film *Symphony in Black*. This collection also includes recordings from radio and television, as well as private recordings from concerts, club and dance dates, and private parties.

For those who do not own the New Sound Planet sets, the out-of-print LP of Holiday in rehearsal, *Billie Holiday Songs and Conversations* (Paramount Records), will be (almost!) enough. Less obsessive collectors will nonetheless want to pick up Holiday's outstanding television recording of "Fine and Mellow," issued on a Pumpkin LP called *The Real Sound of Jazz* (by far preferable to Columbia's *The Sound of Jazz*, which consists not of the performance as it was broadcast but of a rehearsal a few days before). Her "Big City Blues (The Saddest Tale)" by itself is available on Sandy Hook's LP *Black Jazz and Blues: The First Sound Films*. Her "live" set with Count Basie has been issued on a Sagapan LP as *Count Basie at the Savoy Ballroom 1937*. The soundtrack of the Billie Holiday–Louis Armstrong film *New Orleans* is available as an LP on Giants of Jazz.

Acknowledgments

· · ·

My first debt is to Linda Kuehl, the passionate Billie Holiday student who, in the early 1970s, dropped everything and began full-time to collect data about her idol. Kuehl assembled reams of material on Holiday: photos, newspaper clippings, court records, official documents, letters, bankbooks, even shopping lists (Billie was a terrific cook) and set lists scrawled in the singer's broad handwriting to remind her piano player and herself of an evening's anticipated sequence of songs.

Best of all, Kuehl interviewed dozens of people who had known Holiday: fellow musicians, family members, former neighbors, lovers, friends, doctors, lawyers, narcotics agents. Most rare and startling are her interviews with people who lived in Baltimore in the twenties and thirties and remembered Holiday as either Eleanora Fagan or Eleanora Gough. The material Kuehl collected—sometimes sitting in bars, sometimes in Cadillacs in front of bars, and at kitchen tables—sheds new light on parts of Holiday's life that had been shrouded in mystery.

Linda Kuehl died in 1973, her book left undone. Fortunately, upon the recommendation of jazz historian Martin Williams, Toby Byron bought from her family the mountain of Holiday data comprising Kuehl's working file. To Linda Kuehl, with whom I feel a deep kinship, and to her family, I offer thanks. (I should say here that this book is not an updating or revision of Kuehl's; I used her data but not her frame of reference, conclusions, or text.)

To those who knew Billie Holiday and made time for interviews, whether with Linda Kuehl or with me, I extend my gratitude: Willard Alexander, Steve Allen, Vernon Alley, Callye Arter, Al Avola, Eddie Barefield, Lee·Barker, Maisy Barnes, Count Basie, Eddie Beal, Tony Bennett, Johnny Blowers, Oscar Bradley, Mal Braverman, Chlora Bryant, Marie Bryant, Guido Cacianeti, Red Callendar, Mike Cantarino, Robin Carson, Benny Carter, Al Casey, Doc Cheatham, Buck Clayton, Maxwell Cohen, Cozy Cole, Charles "Honi" Coles, John Collins, Bea Colt, Eddie Condon, Willie Cook, Jimmy Crawford, James Cross, Ruby Davis, Dave Dexter, Carl Drinkard, William Dufty, George Duvivier, Milt Ebbins, Billy Eckstine, Harry Edison, Roy Eldridge, Ray Ellis, Jake Erlich, Leonard Feather, Lorenzo Flenoy, Jimmy Fletcher, Helen Forrest, Pops Foster, Hank Freeman, Milt Gabler, Vivian Garry, Mike Gould, Norman Granz, Freddie Green, Tiny Grimes, Lee Guber, Corky Hale, Al Hall, Chico Hamilton, Dr. James Hamilton, Jimmy Hamilton, John Hammond, Bernie Hanighen, Roy Harte, Bobby Henderson, Arthur and Delores Herzog, J. C. Higginbotham, William Hill, Milt Hinton, Fanny Holiday, Kenneth Holdon, Arthur Jarwood, Mrs. Hilton Jefferson, Betty Jerome, George Jessel, Greer Johnson, Walter Johnson, Jimmy Jones, Jo Jones, Lee Josephs, Barney Josephson, Linda Keene, Barney Kessel, Andy Kirk, Irene Kitchings, Chuck Landis, Cliff Leeman, John Levy, John Lewis, Claire and Aaron Liebenson, Melba Liston, Laura "Detroit Red" Livingston, Elain Lorillard, Al Lucas, Lawrence Lucie, Jimmy Lyons, John Magnus, Pigmeat Markham, Herb Marks, Al McKibbon, Carmen McRae, Memry Midgett, Gilbert Millstein, Charles Mingus, Red Mitchell, Toots Mondello, Bob Phillips, Gil Pincus, Specs Powell, Vinnie Puleo, Les Robinson, Gil Rodin, Ned Rorem, Annie Ross, Jimmy Rowles, Jimmie Rushing, Father Scanlon, Frank Schiffman, Joe Schribman, Christine Scott, John Simmons, Art Smith, Elmer Snowden, Alvin Stoller, Robert Sylvester, Sylvia Syms, Billy Taylor, Mel Torme, Irving Townsend, Bobby Tucker, Dick Vance, Sarah Vaughan, Alice Vrbsky, Stan Webb, George Wein, Sid and Mae Weiss, Dickie Wells, Al West, Col. George White, Lee Wiley, Mary Lou Williams, Sandy Williams, Gerald Wilson, Teddy Wilson, Clara Winston, Dorothy Winston, Lee Young, Marl Young, and Earl Zaidins.

To colleagues and friends who may or may not have known Billie Holiday but who helped me to understand her art and her story, I offer thanks: Herbert Hill, Stanley Crouch, Paula Giddings, John Clement, Tom Piazza, Bill Lowe, Mary Gordon, Morris Hodara, Robert Palmer, William Ferris, John Wright, David Blight, Michel and Genevieve Fabre, Hazel Carby, Clarence Walker, S. Marquette Foley, Bernice Johnson Reagon, Nellie McKay, Andrew Szegedy-Maszak, Cholly Atkins, Clarence E. Walker, William Stowe, Werner Sollers, Quandra Prettyman, and Leroy Williams.

For his example and generous intellectual leadership and friendship, special thanks go to Albert Murray.

To my dear friends and comrades, Joseph Reed and Phyllis Rose, who read the manuscript and helped shape its meaning and style, I am deeply grateful.

I also am grateful to the fine research librarians at Barnard College and Columbia University; the Schomburg Center for Research in Black Culture; the Moorland-Spingarn Research Center, Howard University; the James Weldon Johnson Memorial Collection and the Carl Van Vechten Papers, Collection of American Literature, Beinecke Rare Book and Manuscript Library, Yale University; the Hatch-Billops Collection; the Institute for Jazz Studies, Rutgers University; the Performing Arts Research Center at Lincoln Center; New York Public Library, Forty-second Street Branch; the Enoch Pratt Free Library of Baltimore.

Thanks to Barnard student researchers Anne Jamison, Shobha Varughese, Megumi Yamamoto, and Soo Ji Min.

To Barnard College, which supported my research with a sabbatical leave and in countless other ways, I offer my thanks. For its generous support, I am pleased to acknowledge the John Simon Guggenheim Foundation.

To my mother, Ethel B. O'Meally, who did some of the library research for this book and is a constant source of encouragement and inspiration to me, I give thanks.

To my partner and best friend, Jacqueline Malone, I am, again, profoundly in debt.

R. O.

·   ·   ·

Most special thanks must go to Martin Williams and Albert Murray:

Martin, for first mentioning to me the existence of Linda Kuehl's papers, for providing leads that helped me to locate her voluminous research, and for the inspiration of his writings over the years; Albert, for recommending Bob O'Meally as the writer for this book and for his unerring spiritual guidance through the world of jazz. Albert is a beacon, and his generosity of time in setting me straight has been invaluable.

Thanks to Jimmy Monroe, for his time and devotion to Billie Holiday.

Thanks to Jeannette Seaver, Dick Seaver, Cal Barksdale, Jane Donahue, and Allison Davis at Arcade Publishing for all their commitment and patience.

Thanks to Wayne Rosso and Rob Pennock for helping to get the word out.

To Eric Baker, my friend, and his staff, Patrick Seymour and Susi Oberhelman (you're the greatest!).

In addition to the many people Bob has already mentioned, others along the way contributed to the creation of this book. Without their generosity of time and energy, this book could not have been possible: Linda's family (particularly Myra Luftman and her mother, Mrs. Lipnack), Alice Vrbsky, Benton Levy, Chris Albertson, Bob Shamis, Sheldon Greenbaum, Matthew Seig, Mal Waldron, Milt Gabler, Carmen McRae, Buck Clayton, Nancy Elliot, Lorraine Gordon, Rhonda Harrision, Dan Morgenstern and the ever-valuable Institute of Jazz Studies at Rutgers University, Mif Hayes, Phil Schaap, Gary Giddins, Peter Matson, Nan Wise, Francis Paudras, Todd Berry, Steve Byron, Yasmin Byron, Miranda Ottewell, and Barbara Jatkola. Rick Saylor—thank you mightily for your special commitment, editorial skills, and humor.

My efforts herein are dedicated to Lilian and Bryna Fitzgerald and the memory of Lindsay Gaye Rothchild.

T. R. B.